QUICKSILVER

1. In my school uniform and proud of hat

Quicksilver

The Autobiography of
Marie Rambert

MACMILLAN
ST. MARTIN'S PRESS

First published 1972 by
MACMILLAN LONDON LIMITED
London and Basingstoke
Associated companies in New York Toronto
Dublin Melbourne Johannesburg and Madras

Library of Congress catalog card number 72–83628

SBN 333 08942 1

Printed in Great Britain by
W & J MACKAY LIMITED
Chatham

To
Ashley
for the past

to
Norman Morrice
for the future

LIST OF ILLUSTRATIONS

ILLUSTRATIONS

ILLUSTRATIONS

FOREWORD

I HAVE talked so much in my long life that an eternity of silence will not make up for it. I talked to friends, and we laughed together. And we cried together too. I have spoken on the radio and television, and above all in countless interviews with journalists and authors, who have been interested in my career and my company, and particularly in my unique experience of working alone with Nijinsky during his most creative period. For this reason some of what I shall say here may appear slightly familiar to a few readers.

But here is the story of my whole life told in my own words.

Movement, perpetual movement was my element. I crawled very fast on all fours, I ran very fast on all twos, I stood on my head, kicking the while for more fun. Ludwika, my nurse, used to call me 'Quicksilver', and when I was old enough to climb trees I was also nicknamed 'Squirrel'. When I wasn't doing anything else I turned cartwheels. All this was in the country, where we went for long holidays about an hour out of Warsaw, my native city. It seems to me it was always very hot in the summer – but all children remember the summer as very hot. Pine-trees have remained my favourite trees with their powerful vivifying smell. But I loved birches too, though they were not so good for climbing. For picking mushrooms or gathering fir cones one went deep into the forest, and the memory is still alive in me of the wonder of those trees and their intoxicating smell.

One of my earliest memories is sitting opposite my grandmother. Probably I was on a high stool, otherwise how could I see her so clearly, and her face on the same level as mine? She is trying to give me a tiny new potato, swimming in butter, on a spoon. I loved this food, but the desire to tease my granny was stronger, so each time she held the spoon across the table, I said: 'No, I don't want it.' Thereupon she would withdraw the spoon. I at once said: 'Oh yes, I do want it.' The game went on for quite a time, more teasing than eating, but it must have amused my grandmother too, because we laughed all the time.

Another very early memory: I am walking in a field with

my elder sister, and we are gathering flowers. She picked a clover and told me it was good to eat. So I pulled off the petals one by one, imitating her, and bit off the white part inside, which was most delicious. Another time, probably a year or two later, I remember we were trying to catch a squirrel. For a long time it kept us running as it skipped from one tree to another. Eventually I climbed a tree to frighten the squirrel down, and by some miracle my sister caught it and was bitten on her hand so that it bled. Perhaps it was because of this that I was called Squirrel, I can't remember.

Later, still in the country, when I was about six, I went with a boy to catch frogs. I bent over the edge of a pond and tried to catch one. The boy was bending over me trying to hit my lovely frog with a stick. In the end I fell in and caught hold of his knickers to save myself, but pulled him in instead. We floundered in the awful slime of the pond and might well have drowned had not someone seen us from the other side of the pond and pulled us out. Though summer, it must have been a cold day, for I remember I was wearing a red petticoat with white flowers, and it was made of flannelette. I was given a hot wash, but the boy's parents punished him by making him wear his slimy clothes all day.

I remember myself more in the country, probably because I felt happier in the fields and forests than in the crowded flat in town. There were sometimes fêtes in the open air, lit by Chinese lanterns, and there was dancing to fiddles on a platform, and people let off fireworks. I adored the dancing to intoxication. I also remember the joy of riding on top of the peasant haycarts. The return journey in the empty cart was torture, but still fun. Sometimes we ventured out to another village. Remembering now the dust the horses raised makes me reconciled to our modern roads, hideous though they are.

We spoke Polish at home, but when Mother's relations came from the other side of the frontier, we spoke Russian with them. In fact, many years later when I met my Aunt

Pierrot, we tumbled into Russian whenever we were by ourselves.

My father was born in a small town in Poland, of Jewish descent. He was a bookseller, selling mainly schoolbooks, and we lived in a flat near the bookshop not far from the centre of Warsaw. I remember very well the night of the coronation of Nicholas II of Russia in November 1894 when I was six years old. I was brought out that evening on to the balcony, and saw in the Theatre Square, not far away, a huge and very ornamental H II picked out in gas lights (H is the Russian N). But my strongest memory of that night is the smell of the little oil-lamps like night-lights around the bottom of the balcony, for we all had to put up decorations for the occasion.

My father's original family name was Rambam, but he and his brothers were registered by their father each under a different name, in order, I suspect, to appear as only sons and thus escape the heavy three years' military service. One brother retained the original name; my father's was changed to Ramberg, another brother's to Rambert (which I took for the stage), and the last one – would you believe it? – Warszawski! And the bribes for all this were customary, and not even exorbitant.

At that time the custom of bribing was quite prevalent, and the police were very easy. Even some of our school teachers were not averse to taking bribes. Thus one of our pupils who found history very difficult and was afraid of failing at the exams got her mother to see Alexander Alexandrovich Koyalovich. The mother went armed with two banknotes of fifty roubles each. She begged him to help her daughter by coaching her privately and asked how many lessons she would need. He answered: 'I could give her fifteen short lessons at five roubles each, or five longer ones at fifteen roubles each, or even one very thorough one, after which she could not fail – and that will cost you seventy-five roubles.' She reluctantly brought out the two notes without of course daring to ask for change. She somehow imagined that he would ask for a round sum, like fifty roubles or a hundred, and was unprepared for seventy-five.

It is a most extraordinary thing, but I cannot remember ever having been kissed by my mother. Yet I am sure that she was warm-hearted, and my father was kindness itself. I suppose it was perhaps because we were a large family, and when I was a year old my mother had already another child to look after. Anyhow, that is how I try to explain this most extraordinary situation to myself.

Many years later, in fact when I was twenty, mother came to stay with her sister, my aunt with whom I lived in Paris. We became great friends then, and I came to admire her brilliant intelligence. She also recited no end of poetry – she loved it as much as I do, and I think it is from her I inherited my memory for verse. I know reams of it and bore my friends now by reciting on all occasions, and at length, too.

I was much more attached to the servants than to my parents, and I think they too were very fond of me, probably because I was vivacious and affectionate, and was always rushing into the kitchen.

I never cease to wonder how we could have treated the maids as abominably as we did. I remember clearly that I never thought of them as equals, in spite of having had such friendly relations with them. There were no laws relating to their service; they just worked the whole day and the whole week and the whole year. When a new maid came to be interviewed by my mother, she had to bring a booklet of testimonials from all her previous employers. She, poor thing, could not read them. Some of them wrote very long notices, others merely said: 'Slut' or 'Hard-working but a thief'. The maids not only kissed my mother's hand, but often the hem of her dress. It seems to me quite incredible that I saw it with my own eyes. And yet at the same time we were friends, and when I was a little older, I used to write their letters to their parents, which invariably started with the words, 'In the first words of my letter let Jesus Christ be praised. Dear parents. . . .'

Sometimes the letter was (I guess it now) to a lover, and she was shy and dictated incomprehensible nonsense, after which she asked me to add a little doggerel, such as:

> 'As many leaves as there are on the tree,
> As many drops as there are in the sea,
> As much happiness and sweetness
> To Staś, Kasia wishes.'

I once suggested to one of them that I should teach her to read, but it proved, in spite of her goodwill and mine, an absolutely impossible task. She had never learnt anything, she had just worked from childhood. And she was not a special case. It was the same with all of them.

When I went to school I had to wear a very severe brown uniform. They were only strict about it when we were actually in the school. Out of doors we could wear what we liked. So I had my first real hat made specially for me. It was very big and splendid, and was made of Florentine straw with a red taffeta frill all round it. The frill was pinked, so that it stood up like little teeth, and in the centre was a great rose, also made of red taffeta. I was immensely proud of this hat, and I could not wait to wear it on the way to school. Then the day came when I was to go to the photographers, and I wore my hat for the occasion, thinking how marvellous that everybody would see me in it. But when we got there, and I stood in my enormous hat in front of the camera, the photographer said: 'You can't be photographed in that. Nobody will be able to see your face.'

'Oh well,' I said, 'if I can't wear my hat I'm not going to be photographed at all!'

So in the end I was photographed holding it proudly in my hand.

Poland was then part of the Russian empire, and the school I went to was the equivalent of a grammar school here, and was called a Guimnasia in Russian. It was a State institution run by civil servants, who were all Russians, except the teacher of Polish. All subjects were taught in Russian, with the object of forcing russification upon that very recalcitrant Poland. Most of us were bilingual right from the beginning, but we were frightened of being caught speaking Polish at school.

We were taught languages very well, and specially very good French. In the French lesson we were encouraged to speak French as much as possible. We recited French poetry, and I still know by heart long passages of Corneille, Racine, Victor Hugo and others. I also know poems by Goethe and Schiller.

But in the Polish lessons we were forbidden to speak Polish. The lesson was all in Russian – the final outrage. The *directrice* used to come and spy on us. She would listen at the door to make sure we were speaking Russian. We even had to call our Polish mistress, not by her surname, like any other Pole, but by her Christian name and patronymic as if she were a Russian. Of course, the Polish literature itself had to be in the original Polish, and so I can still recite Mickiewicz's great epic poem, *Pan Tadeusz*.

But it was the teacher of Russian literature who always enthralled me. In that very bureaucratic establishment he, Dimitri Porfirievich Yankovsky, managed to teach in a completely unconventional, original way. We read aloud in class great Russian masterpieces – hence the reams of Pushkin and Lermontov stored in my memory. We also read the *Iliad* (in a superb Russian translation by the poet Gniedich, much better than Pope's), the *Odyssey* and the *Æneid*. After making us read aloud a chosen passage and explaining the grammar,

2. My mother

3. My father

4. Myself (on the right)
with my two elder sisters

5. At sixteen

6. Dimitri P. Yankovsky   7. Emile Jaques-Dalcroze

8. Enrico Cecchetti

MY THREE MASTERS

he gave us a dictation relating to it. We never had grammar as a separate subject. In addition to that he encouraged us to learn at home poems of our own choice, and sometimes allowed us to recite them in class.

As I write now I suddenly find a solution to a problem I never could solve before: how was it that Yankovsky was allowed so much freedom in his teaching? Just this minute I have found the answer: he was not merely one of the teachers, he was also the Headmaster of the school! And to think that all those years I never related the two facts! When I was twelve he gave me a photograph of himself on which he wrote: 'To a most excellent pupil and a kind heart.' Of course I treasure it – no one ever again said such things of me and, anyhow, I loved him. Nor did I really deserve the second qualification, for I wrote a wicked satire deriding his drunken habits, a perpetual subject of laughter amongst the pupils, though we all worshipped him. The poem had in all twelve lines written in imitation of Gniedich's Greek hexameters. The first line was:

'The wrath, oh goddess, sing of Dimitri son of Porphyry.'

We had of course all the other usual subjects. I found them all easy and liked them, and I liked the school. But I never really worked at any of them, and so I never learnt to concentrate on one subject – a thing I still find very difficult.

All this work required five lessons daily, sitting absolutely still – quite unbearable to me. In addition to the teacher who sat at his desk, we always had a governess known as the 'Klassnaya Dama', sitting at a little table and taking notes on our conduct, attention and application. She gave marks for each of these, and mine were invariably shocking. (What injustice it was to accuse me of lack of attention! I was all ears for the teachers, and that was why I could dispense with work.) Once when she was ill she was replaced by another, quite old, woman, who wore a false chignon. Nowadays false hair is in fashion, but at that time it was considered a shameful thing. She was a little deaf, and one day while we were walking along the corridor behind her, we gently pulled out one pin after another till the chignon fell off. We, of course, scattered, and she could not complain about such an embarrassing thing. But I know that I felt bitterly ashamed of it quite soon afterwards.

Another misdeed, when I was just about fourteen. We had a new teacher of geography, a charming-looking young man, but obviously one who had never taught girls before. At that time I wore my hair in a long plait. One day during his lesson I threw it forward over my shoulder. He noticed it and did not seem to be able to avert his eyes. After a while I pushed the plait back again. Then out of devilment, I brought it forward again. Again his eyes were riveted to it. He was quite miserable and more shy than ever. The other girls tried to induce me to continue that cruel – though I must say, innocent – game, but I hope I did not.

The teachers all wore navy blue. The women had very severe long dresses with high collars. The men had an almost military uniform in their frock coats with stand-up collars.

The *directrice* who was responsible for our discipline, was a handsome white-haired woman. I suppose she was made up, because she looked very white and pink. We called her Madame Pompadour or Catherine the Great.

We were not allowed to sit down for lunch. It was our exercise period, and we had to eat our sandwiches as we walked up and down a long corridor. Madame Pompadour used to walk up and down it too, and every time we met her we had to stop munching and drop her a curtsey. When it was not deep enough for her liking, she would stop us and we had to curtsey again.

The king of all teachers was to me Wazlaw Slowacki, who came from the Warsaw Opera, where the great Cecchetti was at that time Ballet Master. He gave us dancing lessons in the enormous school hall with its full-length portraits of the Tsar Nicholas II and his beautiful Empress. One of the other pupils wrote a poem about these lessons which brings it all back to me, though she did not share my enthusiasm for dancing, in fact she despised it. Here is a lame translation of some of it:

'On Friday, as usual,' she wrote, 'dancing is the third lesson. The pupils pair off, and walk with small steps towards the hall. On the way the Klassnaya Dama reminds each of us how we should behave. But as soon as her voice is out of ear-shot, nobody listens to her. Dancing and laughing we burst into the hall and take our places. But what has happened? We wait and wait, the Klassnaya Dama patrols outside talking to Madame Pompadour, but still Mr Slowacki doesn't appear. Suddenly we see a green tailcoat at the turn of the steps and Mr Slowacki walks in smartly. Behind him drags the pianist, who turns over in his mind what he will have to play. His ears hang down, his eyes stick out, his mouth goes from ear to ear, but – on the whole – a good soul. They come in. Mr Slowacki bows deeply to the Klassnaya Dama. Then he turns and addresses us: "Mesdames . . ."' He always called us girls 'Mesdames'. '"Mesdames, please be so good as to place your feet in the first position. On the count of one, rise on your points, and now, in time to the music: And One, and Two, and One, and Two." After that we have to do *pliés*, *battements* and even strange *changements*. The time drags and drags. Sweat pours from our brows. At last we hear the bell. The Klassnaya Dama bounces in and says: "The bell has already rung." Then we pair off again and are led out like a flock of sheep.'

I was usually paired off with a girl, Brodska, who amused us all by always boasting of her cousin, the 'Wunderkind Artek'. She had every reason to boast, because he became the great Artur Rubinstein.

We wore party slippers and did all the ballet exercises

holding each other's hands in a circle. We managed to do all the fundamental exercises (which are usually done holding on to a barre) and even jumps while we were still in the circle. After this we went on to ballroom dances. These were not simple walzes and polkas, but complicated dances with different steps and figures, such as the Czardas, the Mazurka, the Pas de Zéphyr, Pas d'Espagne, and others. Slowacki often also taught us bits of ballets that he was dancing at the Opera. I adored them and was good at them. One day after I had finished a little dance, he exclaimed: 'This is real dancing, real fire!' and pleaded with the Klassnaya Dama to allow me an extra class – but she was adamant, and two hours a week remained my maximum. And no marks were given for it – it was not considered a subject worthy of them.

Neither at school nor at home was art as a subject ever mentioned. Theatre, literature, yes, but not the visual arts. My father was a great reader, and he and my mother read *War and Peace* and other masterpieces to each other in their sleepless nights, which I had the misfortune to inherit. But I must not complain of this, for it is when I lie awake at night that I go through all the poetry I ever learnt.

On my tenth birthday, in 1898, I was taken to the Warsaw Opera to see *Swan Lake*. At that time the title meant a great deal more than today when it is worn out with too much familiarity. I was enchanted. Those white dancers on the stage seemed to me real birds. But I was not moved, and it certainly did not occur to me that I could ever do what they were doing, any more than that I could fly like a real bird.

Why did I not at that stage clamour to be taught dancing? Nowadays in a case like mine the child would be sent to a dancing school, but in those days there were simply no dancing schools, outside the Opera, and anyway, no one thought of dancing as a profession for the daughter of a middle-class, rather intellectual family. Indeed, one never thought of *any* profession for a woman, though there were exceptional cases.

I had an aunt who about that time went to Paris to study medicine.

And so I went on with my school and twice-weekly dancing classes. But I always danced for myself and often entertained at parties, improvising dances to music or to poems which I recited myself.

On my last holiday before leaving school I was taken abroad for the first time. We went to Kranz on the Baltic coast of East Prussia. The first sight of the sea made an incredible impression on me. To see that immense horizon for the first time made me feel as though I had not seen the world ever before. No one who had been born by the sea can imagine what a revelation its first sight can be.

I swam a lot and made charming acquaintances on the beach. There was a don from Königsberg University with whom I had long talks. I recited many poems to him, and he taught me much about German literature. We formed a wonderful friendship, though I was only fifteen and he thirty-five. One day he vanished, and I only had a solitary postcard from him in which he gave no address. But he wrote: 'To you, dear Fraülein, who glow with such fire for everything that is great, I send my heartfelt good wishes. H.Z.'

In 1904 I finished school with excellent marks for my work which should have given me a gold medal, but the Klassnaya Dama's dreadful marks for conduct ruined it all. I think she really believed me the devil incarnate (not so far from the truth either).

At that time the whole country seethed with revolutionary ideas. Although serfdom had been abolished at the beginning of the nineteenth century, the régime remained completely autocratic. There was no individual freedom, no freedom of the press, no freedom of movement. It was still much as it had been in the 1820s when the greatest Russian poet Pushkin had been exiled from Petersburg and condemned to live for two years in a remote province, in the middle of a forest, mercifully with his old nurse. But everything he wrote was severely censored, he had to control his inspiration, and only his genius drove him to go on writing and break through. The other great Russian poet, Lermontov, was exiled to the Caucasus and made to fight in the most dangerous battles against the lawful population. Dostoevsky was condemned to death for his revolutionary sympathies and reprieved only at the last minute.

Poland was subjected to all the Russian laws. Her greatest poet Mickiewicz could not bear the Russian oppression and went to live in Paris and plot for the liberation from the Russian yoke.

Under the Tsar Nicholas II, who came to the throne in 1894, the tyranny reached its climax. An echo of all these happenings was bound to reach even our quiet school, and we talked in agitated whispers about the latest acts of terror both by the government and the revolutionaries. We heard of a working girl of sixteen who had been severely wounded during a demonstration. She was dying in hospital, and we visited her in turn, taking her fruit and sweets. Her mother shouted curses against the Tsar when her child died. She begged me to go with her to buy the funeral clothes, as I was apparently exactly her size and build. The shop assistant showed us various garments with a kind of train finished with lace which was to hang out of the coffin and show even after it was nailed down – the custom for young girls. But everything was too expensive, as we had only collected the money amongst ourselves in secret. At last the shop assistant showed us a sort of very long apron finished with lace which would show out of the coffin. But the mother exclaimed in horror: 'What will she look like at the Last Judgement with that rich apron in front and just a shirt at the back!' I don't remember what we did in the end, but I know I was measured for the coffin.

We did other secret things too. Some girls were drawn in through their elder brothers at university to help carry illegal propaganda leaflets and drop them into letter-boxes. We used to do it at twilight, and I remember the sensation of burning on my chest as I carried the forbidden things inside my bodice. We also formed a circle for social studies. There was a professor from Warsaw University who came once a week to give us a lecture on political economy (of all incomprehensible things). I hated the subject and understood nothing, though he spoke very well. But I felt I was doing something towards becoming a useful member of the community, which might destroy Tsarism in the future.

Once, when it was my turn to provide the room for the lecture in our flat, we suddenly heard a bell. One of the boys went to the door and was confronted by two policemen, one of whom had a revolver at the ready. They came into the room, and I can still hear the order: '*Ni's miesta!*' ('Not from the spot,' meaning of course, 'Don't budge!') We were all deathly pale with terror. A girl next to me whispered, 'I have a *Spark* on me.' This was a forbidden paper edited in Switzerland by the famous socialist Plekhanov. A boy behind her whispered, 'Swallow it!' All the while the policemen were turning out all the books from the shelves in search of illegal literature. We all thought we would get into the most terrible trouble, but fortunately nothing further happened.

One day, as I was going to see a friend, I stumbled when turning a corner and nearly fell over the corpses of three workmen. I knew they were workmen by their boots with the trousers tucked inside them. Their brains had been bashed out, and their heads were no longer recognisable as such. They had been killed in a demonstration and left there – presumably to frighten others.

I came home hysterical and shouted threats against the ghastly régime that could allow such things. Our maids, who were simple peasants, heard me but were completely bewildered by it all. My parents were naturally anxious. They were alarmed by the prospect of the revolution, but even as a schoolgirl I had always *wanted* the revolution. And this helped to make us strangers to one another. Now they became anxious for my safety, and began for the first time to think about sending me abroad till things calmed down a little, as they vainly hoped they might.

But all this by no means constituted the whole, or even the most important part of my life at that time. I continued to read voraciously, all the Russian and Polish classics and much of Dickens in translation. Hans Andersen had been read to me before I could read myself.

My theatre-going included, besides Polish plays, Ibsen and Hauptmann and several of Shakespeare's tragedies, of which *Lear* shook me most. I also went to all the usual repertory of opera (nowadays the rarest thing with me), and this actually included some Wagner. I even went to concerts. And of course there were the balls, where I danced my soul out. They used to last till the morning. At dawn the lights were put out, the blinds were opened and in wild excitement we would greet the new day with the *White Mazurka*. Once an officer with whom I was dancing clicked his spurred heels and said: 'With your eyes, Mademoiselle, I could light my cigarette!' I was in seventh heaven.

In the middle of all this I saw Isadora Duncan dance for the first time. She was to give a few recitals in Warsaw on the way through to St Petersburg. At first I was very loath to go and see her, because the advance publicity laid such an accent on her nakedness. But just before her last performance, some friends of mine said, 'You *must* go.' So I went and saw her dance, and I was profoundly moved by the beauty of it. At that moment it did not occur to me that dancing would become my career, but I sensed something of great importance to myself in the expressive language of Isadora's dancing. After the performance I had a message from a friend, who was the mother of Wanda Landowska (the famous harpsichord player), asking me to come and see her. As the mother of another artist she must have had some kind of access to Isadora. She told me that Isadora was looking for a sort of companion who would travel with her.

'If you were to go with her,' she said, 'you might be able to pick up some of her knowledge.'

As Isadora had no school at this time, it did seem to be the only way of learning from her. But my parents were already planning to send me to Paris, and Isadora left for St Petersburg the next day.

On the very day in January 1905 when she was dancing there, the first shots of revolution broke out. The priest Gapon led a crowd of unarmed workmen to the Winter Palace to implore the Tsar to better their miserable lot. Machine guns were fired on them and they were dispersed with dreadful casualties. Much later I learnt that Nijinsky had been by chance in that crowd, mercifully unhurt.

On 1 May 1905, a huge demonstration was organised in Warsaw. A school friend of mine who had a great influence on me during our last year at school told me she intended to march in the procession and I agreed to go with her. I put on clean underclothes, for I had no doubt whatever that I would be killed in the street, and marched off in secret terror to form a procession. But as soon as we linked arms with the other marchers all fear vanished, and I sang at the top of my voice. I felt heroic. Suddenly from a side street appeared a detachment of mounted Cossacks with naked sabres in their hands. They rode straight at us. I was dead with terror and could not have moved a step but, linked with the others, I was dragged into an archway, and the gate was slammed behind us just in time to stop a sabre smashing our heads – it got stuck in the gate.

After that there was no holding me. I felt a full-grown revolutionary ready to undertake the most daring feats. Actually I did totally insignificant ones, like carrying messages or forbidden literature.

My parents then firmly resolved to remove me from Warsaw. But in order to avoid any possible resistance on my part they suggested my going to stay in Paris with my aunt, who was by then a doctor, to study medicine. Though I had not the smallest desire to be a doctor, I thought it a most important profession – at least I would feel a 'useful member of the community'. Quite apart from any other considerations the lure of Paris was irresistible. I had no qualms about leaving Warsaw, suddenly realising how futile were my little efforts to better the lot of humanity. And so off I went.

O F THE journey to Paris I remember only one trifling
incident. I travelled with a school friend, a very pretty girl,
and we stopped for an hour or so in Cologne. Two smart
German officers kept passing our window and muttering
compliments. We were longing to reply and have a little
flirt, but of course we did not dare to. As soon, though, as the
train moved we blew them kisses. But we were badly caught:
the train returned into the station – it had only shunted.
The two officers put their heads right inside our window and
said in German: 'It is severely forbidden to throw dangerous
things out of the window.' How confused we were and how
shocked the two nuns in our carriage!

The night before I left I dreamt I was in Paris, and it was
all palaces, palaces of pink marble and blue marble, and it was
all lit by some magical light from huge candelabras. How dis-
appointing then were to me the horrid approaches of the Gare
de l'Est! But when we drove by the Statue of the Republic in
the place de la République and I read the words: 'Liberté,
Egalité, Fraternité', I was thrilled to feel in a free country.
Those words could never even be pronounced in Russian
Poland, let alone engraved on a public monument. When I
went down into the Métro, a few days later, and noticed that
each bench bore the words 'Allez Frères', of course I thought
it was a call to revolutionary action and not merely an adver-
tisement for the firm of Allez brothers.

I was shocked and puzzled to see women in fur coats with
the fur outside – it made them look like animals to me. Of

course, in the cold Warsaw winters we also wore fur coats, but with the fur on the inside. I realised later that it was a new fashion and the height of *chic*.

And when I was taken to the Champs Elysées and saw really beautiful elegant women, such as I had never seen before, in lovely carriages, and the beauty of that magnificent avenue, I felt that Paris was indeed as I had dreamt it.

My aunt was by now married to Dr Marc Pierrot, and they shared their surgery in the rue des Haudriettes. They were a remarkable pair, very much resembling that other pair, the Curies, in appearance and nature as well as in their early struggles with poverty. But, alas, they had no genius. In the life of Madame Curie by her brilliant daughter Eve there is a wonderful evocation of the tender birth of love between her parents, and it reminded me of the Pierrots' relationship. When they first met as students Pierrot fell in love with her. They were both so shy and diffident that she was unaware of it or of her own feelings for a long time, until one day she heard someone whisper as she came in late for a lecture, 'And here is Colombine.' My aunt blushed red hot, but her Pierrot took her hand and comforted her, and from then on their love dared to flourish.

They refused an offer of help to establish a practice in a rich district and took instead a flat in the Quartier des Archives, once the home of the aristocracy but by then abandoned by the wealthy and gone down in the world. It still has beautiful old buildings such as Les Archives, the Musée Carnavalet and the Hôtel de Rohan.

The Pierrots' practice was enormous, but their earnings were miserable. They were to enjoy fifty years of harmonious married life, but in all that time they never had a holiday together. The utmost they could manage was to share one day of a weekend: she would go to the country on Saturday night: he arrived on Sunday morning and they spent the Sunday together till the last train. They used to be called out most nights for confinements. They shared their patients, whom they loved.

My uncle, though the mildest of men, was a follower of Kropotkin – that renegade Russian prince who preached anarchism – and had many friends among that crowd. One day as he was examining the editor of their paper, *Plus Loin*, in his office, the police came in for a search. My uncle said to the Commissaire de Police: 'It's a dirty job you're doing here, sir,' and was promptly arrested and flung into prison. He was released after three days, but he lost his job as insurance doctor by which he used to supplement his meagre earnings. Both he and my aunt gave *les camarades* their services free – and the *camarades* never scrupled to call them out in the night often just for a little comfort. My uncle was devoted to their journal *Plus Loin*, and years afterwards he was still sending copies to my husband, so that Ashley used to exclaim, 'Encore *Plus Loin*' as they dropped through our letterbox.

The Pierrots always treated me as a daughter, though they had two of their own. In fact they were much nearer to me than my own parents.

My aunt found that I was too young to start studying medicine – little knowing how I hated the very thought of it – and so suggested that I should work for the Certificat d'Etudes Françaises – a one-year course at the Sorbonne. I attended the lectures but never did any work at home. I spoke French with the Pierrots' children as well as with their friends and my own, and at the end of the year I had mastered it perfectly. On the day of the written French exam I had lunch at a house of a friend in Passy, and everybody drank to the success of my exam, so I had to drink with them. All my life I have had a very feeble head for liquor, and don't need it to be gay. A liqueur glass of wine is enough to make me giddy, so I felt absolutely drunk – though everybody thought I was pretending. I got to the Métro to go to the Châtelet, from which a bus would take me to the Sorbonne. In the Métro I tried to sing to myself a little French song 'Il était un petit navire' just to be in the right mood (linguistically, so to say) for the exam. But, horror of horrors! not one French word could I utter, it was only Russian or Polish songs that I could hum to myself. However I got out at the Châtelet and took a bus up the Boulevard St Michel. Just before I got to the Sorbonne I went into a little café I knew and announced loudly that I was drunk and asked what I could do to get a clear head for the exam. They gave me some strong coffee, and I rushed across the road to the Sorbonne where a group of friends were waiting anxiously for me, as I was late.

I again announced that I was drunk and could not go in for the exam. I heard myself speak too loud, but could not control it in time. They all said: 'Your French is perfect, you cannot fail. Anyhow Marie will be sitting in front of you with a dictionary, and Charles behind with a Larousse – so don't worry.'

The professor came in and read to us one of Voltaire's *Contes Philosophiques*. I did not take in a word he was saying and put down my pen, as I was sure I could not write a resumé of that story – which was the object of the exam. But after a pause of a few moments he read the story again. I listened with all my might and wrote an excellent résumé, but it included one colossal bloomer. I said, 'Il était *le plus mauvais roi* . . .' Many years later, when I met Professor Régnier at a dinner and told him I had passed an exam with him he remembered that paper and told me how puzzled the committee were at such an unexpected barbarism in the middle of fluent French.

That first year in Paris was, in the main, devoted to a gay student life. We visited museums and monuments and went to some lectures in the daytime and cafés and *boîtes de nuit* at night. I seldom came home before two, and my aunt was quite worried. She told me I was burning the candle at both ends, and it would be burnt out by the time I was thirty. 'Good

Lord,' I exclaimed, 'I hope I will not live to be an old woman of thirty.'

The cabarets on the Montmartre were irresistible: there was one called L'Enfer, where one was served by devils, and one, La Mort, where one ate off a coffin and was served by undertakers. I promptly learned their various *chansons*, and have not forgotten them to this day. On one occasion a friend took me to a cabaret where on a small stage they were showing projections with a magic lantern and inviting members of the audience to come up. My friend volunteered and sat down at a little table looking blankly at the seat opposite him, which was empty. He did not know that on that table was projected a little rabbit. 'Poser un lapin' is a slang expression meaning to fail to come to a promised rendezvous. So he looked like someone who was still waiting for his lady friend. It was very funny. For the next turn, as nobody volunteered, I climbed on to the stage, and immediately a great guffaw went up. I only understood why when they showed the projection alone: a girl sitting in lace knickers and adjusting a garter – but with *my* head. One could not help laughing at oneself in such situations.

A very favourite amusement was to go on bicycles for excursions outside Paris. I loved riding a tandem with some reckless youth in front driving me along at breakneck speed (all of twelve miles an hour).

Soon after I arrived in Paris, my uncle took me to an exhibition of very modern painting – no doubt it was the Salon des Indépendants, and it was full of great impressionist masterpieces. But we hated it heartily, and my uncle said: 'It's a mockery.'

My aunt also took me to see what was billed as Sarah Bernhardt's last appearance – of course, she was to make a few other last appearances later on – but this one was announced as the very last appearance of Sarah Bernhardt in *Phèdre*. When the great Sarah came on to the stage and started speaking I nearly burst out laughing, and so did my aunt – though she was a woman who had very little humour – because the voice sounded so cracked and so funny. Yet after a few seconds you did not hear the crack in the voice, you just heard the golden voice, which was something of incredible beauty. Everything that she was saying became so convincing, and you lived the role so marvellously with her, that you didn't even notice that there were other people on the stage, and that the rest of the play was going on. She had that great quality that one saw in Isadora Duncan and in Pavlova – two people who did not need an intermediary to talk to an audience. They did not need an author, they did not need a choreographer. They could give themselves to the audience direct. This is a very rare and special gift. In Sarah Bernhardt's case it did not matter whether she appeared in Racine or in Rostand, because it was she herself, her own soul, that she gave to us.

I must have seen Sarah Bernhardt more than once, and later I took to imitating her. Once in the dressing-room at Monte Carlo I was amusing the other dancers by giving an imitation of her, when a dresser from another room came rushing in and said: 'On dirait Madame Sarah!' So it became quite a party trick. James Agate, a great admirer of Sarah Bernhardt, once heard me do it, and thereafter, whenever we met anywhere, he always made me repeat it, though my husband hated me showing off in public. Once we were all at a party at Ivor Brown's, and although I had an absolute conviction that not another soul there, besides Agate, wanted me to do the wretched imitation, he positively forced me. So that I had to do it whether I would or not. It was the greatest flop of my life. Everybody was heartily relieved when I stopped.

In Paris in 1905 there was dancing, dancing on every occasion, at balls or in the open air. One night I went to a fancy dress ball in a beautiful Eastern costume. I was asked

9. Pierrot family, 1905. Madame Pierrot is in the centre, I am to her right, and bearded Dr Pierrot in the back row.

10. Natalie Barney's play about Sappho at Neuilly, 1905. The actors from the Comédie Française in the centre. I am second from the right. Penelope, wife of Raymond Duncan, playing the flute, Eva Palmer seated in the centre

11. Isadora Duncan   12. Anna Pavlova

13. Tamara Karsavina

MY THREE MUSES

for the Mazurka by one of the guests, Kurylo, who was a dancer from the Warsaw Opera. He improvised wonderful figures and steps which I followed in a state of ecstasy. Everybody stopped dancing to watch, and it became a real performance. After terrific applause several people came up to congratulate me. Amongst them was – oh, miracle! – Isadora Duncan's brother Raymond. He was a very handsome man dressed as an ancient Greek. This for him was not a fancy dress, but his usual attire. He paid me the most exciting compliments about my dancing and went so far as to say that I danced every bit as well as Isadora. (I think they had had an estrangement for a while, and he was not averse to belittling her.) I begged him to teach me, but he insisted that I was ready for the stage there and then. But how to get on to the stage? He merely said: 'It will come.'

I made great friends with him and his wife Penelope Sikilianos, who was a genuine Greek, and I went to dance for them and their friends quite frequently. He presented me with a little Greek tunic and advised me to discard shoes and go over to sandals, which at that time were quite unknown except on Greek frescoes. I tried to wear them, but balked at wearing the tunic in the street. One day, when I went in my sandals to lunch with a friend in her luxurious flat at Passy, the concierge sent me up by the *escalier de service*. I rang the bell and found myself facing an irate cook who, seeing me in those sandals, was unwilling to believe that I was one of the guests for whom she had cooked a sumptuous meal. She was only convinced when she saw the hostess kiss me and apologise profusely.

I soon abandoned the sandals, but under Raymond's influence I sought unconventional clothes. I bought a big brown felt hat and stripped it of its ribbons: they were unnecessary, therefore ugly, I reasoned. I was pleased with the result and imagined I looked like a Rembrandt portrait. One day when I stood looking in a shop-window I felt something pulling at my hat; a driver of a stationary cab had whizzed his whip round my hat and said: 'There's a trimming for your hat!' – an absurd memory that has long since made up for my discomfiture at the time.

Raymond took me to a beautiful villa at Neuilly, where two very rich American women, Eva Palmer, who later married Raymond's son, and Natalie Barney, lived. There I met Colette Willy. Although she had left her husband and was reputedly living with the actress Polaire, she had not yet dropped her married surname. Much later she began to sign her books simply 'Colette'. It was Polaire who had been chosen to act the part of Colette's heroine Claudine when her novels were first dramatised. Polaire was celebrated for her *taille de guêpe* – twenty centimetres or so – and, apart from the fact that one was fair and one was dark, she and Colette were akin in type, especially as they both cut their hair short – very eccentric at the time. Polaire's was black and fuzzy, and it stood out like a sort of crown, while Colette's was smooth and light.

Colette was very flattering about my dancing, and with her theatrical connections gave me introductions to Madame Rasimi, the manager of a big music-hall, and Wague a celebrated mime. But they wanted me to create a proper programme and show it to them, not just to dance about nothing in particular.

Natalie Barney wrote a play about Sappho which was performed on the lawn at Neuilly. There were actors from the Comédie Française to act the speaking parts. I remember the line: 'Et Sappho de Lesbos où est-elle? Nous ne le savons plus, elle est morte.'

The choruses were sung to what was supposed to be Greek music, played upon pipes, a flute and other suitable instruments. There was a choric hymn beginning: 'Levez haut les poutres, charpentiers, évoé' which I am sure I have seen somewhere else, so I do not think Natalie Barney wrote it, she must have taken it from some classic source and incorporated it into her play.

There were dances, in which I took part, and which Raymond arranged. He did not really arrange anything, for he was not a choreographer, but vaguely told us where to go. We were barefoot and we wore tunics, so everything looked Greek to him.

After the play was over there was a party in the garden, and I was so excited that I jumped across the water on to a little statue of a cupid in the middle of the pond. Then people began to shout to me not to fall in because there was an alligator there. Presumably he was tame, but I hung on to the cupid very tightly all the same.

About this time I saw in a newspaper that Isadora Duncan was going to Warsaw for a series of concerts. Without a moment's hesitation I went by twenty trains from Paris back to Warsaw and went to the Philharmonia where she was dancing. I was absolutely mad with joy to see all that beauty. First she danced *Greek Maidens at Play* to Gluck's music. When Isadora danced you felt as though she was carried by the music without any effort on her part. I had the feeling that it was as easy as walking, and the grace of it was like a bird's flight. She threw a ball, ran after it, bounced it, caught it in mid-air; or else she played with 'osselets' reclining by the sea, leaning on one elbow and throwing up those little square bones from the inside of her hand to the outside. The grace of her movements, the peaceful happiness of her mood together with Gluck's music created a complete world of its own – and yet recognisably antique. Of course she had neither a ball, nor the little bones – but you saw it all in her dance. Later she danced the *Primavera* to a gavotte of Gluck's, strewing invisible flowers and bringing Spring with her movements. Then at the end of the first part she did the *Danse des Scythes* from *Iphigénie en Tauride* in a red tunic, representing a fierce warrior with great leaps and powerful arm movements. There were also in the programme some dances to Schubert and Chopin, and it all finished with a Bacchanale. She was quite alone on an empty stage, with the famous blue curtains Gordon Craig had designed for her as backcloth, wearing a simple little terracotta-coloured tunic, brandishing big branches of fern; and yet not even Bacchus himself with all his train of Maenads could have created a deeper Bacchic mood. The audience got carried away into mad shouts, and she had to repeat the dance again and again. I rushed backstage, pushed aside a tall young man with a leonine mane who was guarding Isadora's door – it was Gordon Craig – and threw myself on my knees kissing her hands with tears streaming down my face. Finally I was torn away from her and ejected. The next day my mother read out a paragraph from the paper about 'a hysterical young girl who forced an entrance into the great artist's room'. I admitted it was me, and for the first time dared to cry out that I intended to dance at all costs.

And when I said 'dance' it meant to me Isadora's dance. What I had seen as a child in *Swan Lake* in Warsaw, probably a rather provincial production, had not really moved me at all. The bodies of the dancers had seemed so rigid, their movements so stilted with their formal poses and fixed smiles. They had stirred in me no desire to dance. It was only much later that I understood what classical ballet meant and what a powerful means of expression it could be.

With Isadora I felt an absolute communion, and it seemed to me I could speak her dancing language.

Next day I went to see Isadora in her hotel. She was resting on a couch, and she interrupted my flood of incoherent words with a very calm talk on what makes a woman happy. She maintained that only love and children brought happiness to a woman and advised me not to venture on to the stage. She never even asked me to show what I could do. The advice she gave stemmed from a deep conviction – motherhood to her was the peak of happiness – but she was also obviously prompted by the most understandable desire to get rid of me quickly. How insolent it was of me to force myself upon her a second time!

After that if ever I was in a city where she was performing, I never failed to go and see her. I grew to admire her ever more and more. Quite apart from her genius as a dancer, she was also a great reformer. She was the first dancer to discard corsets, which at that time every woman wore. (I remember my mother being laced into one by the maid and saying, with a gasp: 'Tighter, Kasia, tighter. I can still breathe!') Isadora not only wore no corset, but I doubt if she wore anything at all except her Greek tunic. In spite of Raymond's advice, I could not follow her in that. Then, of course, there was no scenery for her, just the Gordon Craig curtains – and that was a tremendous innovation in itself.

And, in addition, she brought a completely new repertoire of music. Instead of dancing to the sugary tunes which were considered till then the only ones 'danceable', she composed to the greatest classical music, which to me was quite the most wonderful inspiration for dancing.

Many people, specially those acquainted only with the technique of classical ballet, considered Isadora an amateur, because of the simplicity of her movements. But anybody else, trying to dance those same dances, made no impression at all. She had no need to do any more than she did. She was a genius who spoke to the audience direct by sharing her ecstacy with them. When you saw her dance you felt you were dancing yourself.

Now I became quite resolved to find a way to dance on the stage. I had a great friend called Edmée Delebecque, whose husband was one of my uncle's *camarades*. She was a poet, and introduced me to a whole circle of interesting and cultured people. She had a villa in Grasse in the South of France, and kept inviting me to stay with her. She loved my dancing and wanted to help me, so I accepted her invitation.

On the way from Warsaw to Grasse I took the opportunity

to stop for a few days in Vienna, so that I could visit an old school-friend. She was earning a good living doing instant charcoal drawings as part of a programme in the cabaret Nachtlicht – a bit intellectual and very fashionable. The audience suggested a subject, and she drew it, and very well too. The poet Peter Altenberg, very much in vogue then, was also in the programme. My painter friend insisted on my doing an audition for the manager, and he instantly offered me a good engagement. For once in my life I was cautious. I said I was expected in Paris and would give him a reply in a few days. The truth was that a handsome baritone in the company tried to persuade me that 'chastity is a very overrated virtue', and Altenberg seemed to share his opinion, too. I got alarmed and consulted another friend who happened to be in Vienna at the time. She said that she would rather support me earning her living as a washerwoman than see me appear in cabaret. That decided me, and I refused the engagement.

During those few days in Vienna I managed to see the dancer Ruth St Denis, who was by this time famous. She was appearing in a music-hall and danced Indian-inspired dances most beautifully. Her figure was perfect, her costumes too, and the movements she did, mostly on one spot and chiefly with the arms, had great style. She became the important dancer who, together with her husband Ted Shawn, founded the Denishawn company in which Martha Graham made her début. Ruth St Denis died recently, well over ninety.

As soon as I arrived in Grasse, Edmée and I wrote to Paris for all the books on dancing that existed then – perhaps half a dozen compared with the hundreds that are being published now! As I did not wish to practise my balletic exercises and yet felt a need to do some regular training, I went to a teacher of acrobatics in Cannes. After the first lesson he offered to arrange an acrobatic turn for us both as a music-hall number. I declined this, but enjoyed the practice. At the same time I began to work seriously on a programme.

Edmée influenced me in other ways. Besides being a poet (she had published two volumes of verse and had made a beautiful translation of the Psalms) she was an excellent pianist. Once when she was playing a Beethoven sonata – not the sort of thing that one would normally dance to – I began improvising dances, and flung myself into it with such ecstasy that she said: 'You are just like Myriam the prophetess dancing with joy after the children of Israel had crossed the Red Sea. I shall call you Myriam from now on.'

Here comes another muddle: although my birth certificate bears the name Cyvia, I was never called by it, but by the pet name Cesia. When I came to Paris nobody could pronounce it – they made it sound very ugly like 'ces chats', which aggravated me – so we all adopted Edmée's suggestion. They always pronounced my surname Rambert, even when spelt with a 'g', so when I came to London I changed it altogether to the more elegant Marie Rambert. But all my friends call me Mim to this day.

Edmée introduced me to Alice and Yvonne Diéterle, her great friends, who also became mine. They were the daughters of a painter, an Academician, who lived with his family in a beautiful house called 'La Ferme des Roses' – quite rightly too – at Criquebeuf in Normandy. Alice was a splendid pianist, while Yvonne was a sculptress. A large barn in the yard at 'La Ferme des Roses' had been transformed into a studio. I stayed with the Diéterles for several months, and every day I went to work in the studio with Alice who played any music I wanted. The first piece I chose was Schubert's *Moment Musical*. I always practised in the little green tunic that Raymond had presented me with, and of course barefoot. Yvonne, who was used to very static Paris models for her sculpture, was enchanted to find a dancing one. She did endless drawings and was most enthusiastic about my work. As her father was a fashionable painter, they had an enormous circle of friends in the world of art whom they used to invite to see me practise. These included two sons of Jean-Paul Laurens, both successful painters, and Georges Desvallières.

One day Yvonne told me of a cousin, a painter who was longing to see me dance, but I didn't catch the name. And we were not introduced beforehand because I was already dressing then. I danced, and I noticed sitting with them a figure in a black cape and a black velvet beret – this was the uniform of painters at that time, just like long hair later on. When I had finished dancing the painter came up and congratulated me: 'Mademoiselle, mais c'était la chose la plus merveilleuse du monde . . . unique . . .' and so on.

I just gasped out my thanks: 'Merci, monsieur. Merci, monsieur.'

Then my friends began to laugh, and I realised that it was not a *monsieur* at all – not a *cousin* but a *cousine*. When I was dancing I was so carried away that I didn't know what was happening around me. They could put anything across me.

When I was in Paris I did all my rehearsing in a large room which a friend of mine, Pauline Rumeau, lent me in her house. She loved the repertoire which I had built up by that time and assured me that I needed only to show myself to the public to be flooded with engagements at once. So she invited some two hundred guests ('only our intimate friends'), had a stage built in the drawing-room, and there I was to make my début.

The long-awaited evening came at last. There was a brilliant assembly, which I surveyed in great trepidation through a keyhole: lots of women in terrific *décolletés* whom I heartily envied, being very skinny myself.

First on the programme there was a singer, mildly applauded, then a comic, obviously more to their taste, then poor me, with my interpretations of Schubert and Chopin. They hardly gave me a hand after the first dance, but towards the end they warmed up thoroughly. In fact a lot of them insisted on being introduced and congratulated me very warmly.

After midnight when they had all gone, Pauline said: 'You see how they all loved it and how enthusiastically they applauded you.'

I retorted that they only did so out of politeness to her. Thereupon she offered to ring up any person I chose from the audience and let me listen in to the reply on an extra pair of earphones she had. I chose a woman who had sat in the front row, very beautiful and conscious of it, and who had looked at me rather with contempt, I thought. The conversation went like this:

'How did you like the little dancer?'

'Very good, very good.'

'Please tell me sincerely what you think of her, for her parents are against it, and we must not encourage her unless she is worth it.'

'She is a very good dancer indeed. Plain, of course, but she has *chic*.'

Pauline was distressed, but I was quite undismayed. I preferred to be called plain and complimented on my dancing rather than the other way round.

That evening at Pauline's resulted in several invitations to dance at private soirées, and I began to make a living. I charged a hundred francs, though I didn't always get it. The ladies of the Faubourg St Germain were prepared to spend money on food, flowers and drink, but not always on a fee for me as well. A hundred francs seemed to them exorbitant.

'Look, darling,' they would say, 'I have my decorator, my confectioner, my florist, without counting the champagne – all this for your sake. And then you come and ask for a fee as well (100 francs!). How can I possibly pay you all that? You are too young!'

'It is just because I *am* young,' I would answer, 'and I must continue to study, that I need it.'

One of them, after my rehearsal at her house, asked me to leave my little tunic with her. 'It's a little bit crumpled,' she said, 'I should like to have it ironed.' But actually she thought the tunic was not rich enough for her grand party. To my horror, on the day of the performance a copy of it, in a most expensive and unsuitable material, was given to me at the last moment. What could I do but dance miserably? Afterwards I made a scene with Madame la Comtesse that she can't have forgotten in a hurry.

Pauline encouraged artists to draw me, though when Marguerite, her housemaid, saw one drawing of me done by a young painter, she just said: 'It is Mademoiselle, all right, you can see that at once. It is Mademoiselle's hat.' She was a Breton girl whom Pauline had recently engaged, and she had just learnt that when the lady pressed the bell, she, Marguerite, had to come. Once when she was dusting a picture, she dropped it and frantically rang the bell to call her mistress to help her.

At one party the great Clemenceau saw me dance. When I had finished I was introduced to him. No doubt he had imagined me much taller (as dancers always look on the stage), for he looked at me and said, 'C'est tout ça, la danseuse?' And then, as if to excuse himself, 'Oh, vous paraissez plus grande sur la scène.'

I was flattered to have been spoken to for the first time in my life by such an illustrious personage. Yet, as a matter of fact, he was a very small man himself.

Madame Rosnoblet, one of the hostesses for whom I danced, once took me to Paderewski's house at Morges near Lausanne in Switzerland. I stayed the night there, and in the morning I remember listening, transported, to his two hours' practice at the piano. There was a huge house party, and I was to be Paderewski's treat for his guests – which was no small honour. When I had finished dancing Paderewski presented me with a beautiful pendant – an enamel swan with little emerald eyes and a topaz for a beak. I treasured it, but lost it in a field within the year.

During my second year in Paris I was befriended by Madame Aurore Lauth-Sand, a very distinguished woman, wife of a painter and granddaughter of George Sand. She was very beautiful, and a lovely amateur dancer, specialising in Spanish dancing. She once gave a marvellous party, to which Zuloaga and other Spanish painters came, and a Spanish woman danced so seductively that one of the audience suddenly burst out: 'I want her.'

Aurore eventually persuaded me to have lessons in ballet even if I didn't like it, because she maintained it would give me a better status than to be a barefoot dancer only. So I went to classes given by Madame Rat of the Paris Opéra. Rat really was her name, improbable though it sounds, especially since it is also the name given to the beginner class at the Grand Opéra; those little girls with rat-like pigtails whom Dégas loved to paint were known as 'les petits rats'.

Madame Rat was a real French *petite bourgeoise* if ever there was one. She was a very bad teacher, and with her I was a very bad pupil. I was taking these lessons *à contre-cœur*, for I didn't believe in the system she used, and she couldn't interest me in her type of movement. I particularly disliked the *porte de bras* of the French Academy. Later when I was taught Italian arms by Cecchetti I realised that it was possible to have beautiful arm-movements in classical ballet. And later still the arm-movements, under the influence of the Russian Bolshoi and Kirov, became even more beautiful.

Madame Rat used to boast of her wonderful instep, and amused me with all the gossip of the Paris Opéra. She loved to talk about the weather, but it was quite impossible to get her to agree with you. If I should say, 'It is cold today', she would reply, 'No, dear, it is only the *fond de l'air* which is cold. Actually it is quite warm.'

The next day I would say, 'How warm it is!' And sure enough she corrected me again: 'No, the wind is warm, but the air itself is cold.'

Then Georges Desvallières, the painter whom I had met at the Diéterles', invited me to dance at the opening of the following season's Salon d'Automne, of which he was President. The Salon d'Automne was an annual exhibition of new pictures, and my friends thought that to dance on such an occasion would be a wonderful way of being launched on a career of dancing recitals. I eagerly began to work on a programme when disaster overtook me. I became violently ill with appendicitis.

Before they could operate, I had to starve completely for about a month, otherwise there was danger of peritonitis. Recovering from the operation was a long business. At that time they kept you lying flat and all bandaged for at least three weeks. At last I was allowed to sit up, which made me dizzy, but after an hour or so I stole out of my room and wandered down the passage. I had not seen myself in a mirror for more than two months. Usually one sees one's reflection involuntarily many times a day in a passing shop-window or a mirror, and so never has a *first* impression of one's own face. Out of the passage I stumbled into the nurses' sitting-room and looking up saw myself by chance in the mirror. The first thought that flashed through my mind, before seeing myself *as myself*, was: 'How like my mother!' It was a curious sensation. Immediately afterwards I thought: 'Not half as plain as I imagined!' I had gone very thin and my eyes looked enormous. In one of my dreams during my long fast I had eaten a turkey stuffed with a goose and some other very tasty bird. In another I was tall and blonde!

It took me a long time to recover, for during that enforced immobility adhesions formed and every movement caused me pain. Nowadays all this would be avoided, but through this wretched appendicitis I lost my opportunity to dance at the Salon d'Automne.

Pauline's father-in-law, Monsieur Rumeau, often used to visit me in hospital. He adored me, and as I was young and not above exploiting his affection for me, I got him to start teaching me English, though I dread to think with what accent. He was a Marseillais, and his accent in French was already bad enough.

He taught me from a book by a man named Robertson, and I can remember exactly how it was laid out. There would be a short passage of some six or seven lines of English. I remember one that began: 'We are told that the Sultan Mahmoud by his perpetual wars abroad, and his tyranny at home, had filled the dominions of his forefathers with ruin and desolation and had unpeopled the Persian Empire.' Underneath each word there would be its literal translation into French, thus: 'Nous sommes dits que le sultan Mahmoud, par ses perpétuelles guerres au dehors . . .' And finally there was the translation into good French: 'On nous dit . . .' Thus you had a clear idea of the relative construction of English phrases and French. It was a simple, but brilliant system. I was interested, and I learnt it all by heart in no time.

At the very end of the book there was an extract from *Childe Harold*, 'Adieu, adieu! my native shore . . .' This gave me my first taste of Byron. I already knew that he was the hero of Pushkin and Lermontov, so I longed to read him in the original. But it was not until much later that somebody gave me *Childe Harold* and I learnt long passages from it and from *Manfred*. Meanwhile, I learnt four sonnets of Shakespeare in the original, having previously known them by heart in the perfect French translation by François Victor Hugo, son of the great poet. They were not rhymed but retained marvellously the rhythm and feeling of the original, and now I know forty of them, which I can recite in the middle of the night. Monsieur Rumeau thought me very foolish to waste my time learning lots of words and phrases that would be of no use in everyday life – for he was a typical *rentier*.

I had been operated on by the famous surgeon Dr Walter, who was also surgeon to Madame Curie, which made me feel very proud, especially as he did all the dressings himself. When I was well again my aunt advised me to go and see him to thank him personally for all his kindness and ask him what I owed. He smiled, kissed me on the cheek and said: 'Here are my fees!'

Not long after my operation my aunt had to go and stay in Tunis, to recover from an illness, and during that time I lived at a sort of girls' club called Amicitia – it would not have been considered *comme il faut* for me to remain in the flat with my uncle while his wife was away.

One evening when I was having dinner with two of the girls they talked all the time about food and its delights. I stopped them indignantly: 'You talk like old old men who have lost all other pleasures in life!'

Whereupon Suzanne exclaimed: 'Qu'est-ce que vous voulez, mon petit? – On se volupte comme on peut!'

A Swiss girl at Amicitia called Alice Hofman was very enthusiastic about my dancing. She suggested that I might like to go with her to Geneva and take part in a ten-day summer holiday course at the Jaques Dalcroze Institute.

'Of course, you don't *need* Dalcroze,' she said. 'But it would be interesting for you to see what he does.'

So I went, I saw, and stayed for three and a half years.

W E ARRIVED in Geneva on a Sunday night, and the first sight of the snow-clad mountains brought tears to my eyes. Once again, as when I first saw the sea, I was overwhelmed by this new vision of the world. I could not believe that those white clouds were in reality solid mountains supporting the sky. Its immensity quite overawed me, and I felt as though I perceived the infinite.

The next day I went to the first lesson. I intended to take two or three classes out of the six given each day, but I took them all for I became so carried away that I did not feel the least bit tired. Dalcroze was a short man with the stomach already beginning to stick out, a pointed beard and turned up moustaches. He was a genius at teaching. Whatever subject he taught, whether it was movement to music, or *solfège*, or improvisation at the piano – he made it the most interesting subject on earth and carried you away with his enthusiasm. And when he felt we were getting exhausted he came out with some joke so funny that we shook with laughter and felt fresh again. He always obtained from us more than we thought we could give – which is what I hope my pupils may say of me one day.

I had only intended to stay for the ten-day course. But he took me into the school, and let me stay without paying, eventually to become a teacher there. I found all the subjects difficult, even the movement to music, as this had to be done not spontaneously, but with different objects in view. We had to run twice as fast or twice as slowly as the music, or stop suddenly at the word of command 'Hop!' for a certain number of bars, then at the word 'Hop!' change the running step to skipping, and so on. I felt tied in knots but kept on trying.

Dalcroze had begun as a teacher of harmony and *solfège* at the Conservatoire in Geneva. He noticed that people when singing were inclined to speed up or slow down according to their temperament, but when singing and *marching* at the same time they kept a perfect tempo. On this basis he founded a very precise system of teaching rhythm. There was already a precise system of teaching harmony and melody. But rhythm as a separate subject was a discovery of Jaques Dalcroze. There had never been before him any training specifically in rhythm – that essential constituent in music. He invented a series of conventional movements to represent all the time-values and, thanks to our lessons in *solfège*, also to the melody. It was called *gymnastique rythmique*. Several conductors came to study rhythm with him.

Yet all this did not amount to dancing, not only because the conventional gestures and movements lacked beauty but above all because there was no underlying technique of movement as such. Dalcroze's object was emphatically not the dance, but movement as a means to study rhythm. He often reproached me with being too balletic in my interpretations. 'Tu es trop extérieure,' he would say.

Practically all the pupils at the Institute were musicians, some of them quite elderly. They could all beat me in musicianship. Many of them had the perfect or absolute pitch – highly prized, of course. Dalcroze invented excellent exercises to improve it, so as to obtain at least what he called 'a *relatively* absolute pitch'. One day when explaining this he added, turning to me: 'But yours is *absolutely* relative.'

When a pupil came in late and stealthily tried to join the class, Dalcroze would alter the rhythm he had been playing and accompany the stealthy steps – thus revealing the poor culprit who found himself dancing his embarrassment. He always improvised at the piano. We had to stand in a circle and listen and try to understand all the details of the music and suddenly, at the word 'Hop!' interpret it. There was a delightful grey-haired couple in the class, Freiherr Otto von Lubecke and Freifrau Gertrude von Lubecke. Like all the other pupils they wore only a black bathing costume and had bare arms and legs. Of course they looked funnier than most of us, but were not in the least self-conscious about it. The Freiherr had one bugbear: the word 'Hop!' In his anxiety to start on 'Hop!' in time he always started too soon. After stopping him more than once Dalcroze said, 'Ah, le petit indiscipliné!' and that darling Freiherr laughed with us all – and then started again too soon.

We had to call out the key when there were modulations in the music which Dalcroze improvised. One day somebody blew his nose in the midst of it and Dalcroze called out: 'Fa triple bemol' (meaning that it was the key of F treble flat).

Dalcroze was a brilliant musician; he was a genius at improvisation – that was the means by which he taught his method. He was always experimenting. I found improvisation at the piano very difficult. In my childhood I had about three terms of once-weekly piano lessons and simply could not play. With Dalcroze we were called out one after the other to the piano on a little platform and had to improvise in a given rhythm and key. He had the diabolical humour to give titles to these themes. Thus, when a Swiss girl, who seemed to have more milk than blood in her veins, went up he said: 'Allons, Simone, quelque chose de sanglant intitulé Caligula.'

Or to Fraülein Zimmermann, a very shy German girl: 'Your theme is "Eduard – Ich habe Angst."' (Edward, I am terrified.)

Or to me:

'Viens, toi la sombre, la passionnée, donne-nous Clytemnestre!'

Once when he had teased me beyond endurance I burst into

tears and rushed out. For a few days I never went up to kiss
him in greeting or at the end of the day as we all did. I came
to class regularly, but avoided talking to him. Then I met
him by chance in the street. As he was coming up to me he
took out his handkerchief, put it to his eyes and pretended to
cry bitterly. Who could resist kissing him immediately? And
his charm extended to the written word too. He once wrote
to me: 'La maîtresse d'Emile (qui est aussi celle de gymnastique) viendra te chercher vendredi . . .'

Although Dalcroze's subject was music and he taught it
magnificently, it was his quality as pedagogue that influenced
me above all. Like his compatriot Pestalozzi, he was a builder
of character, and it was thanks to him that I learned to work
hard.

During the first Christmas holidays he asked us to write an
essay on any subject we chose, and I wrote – it staggers me
now to think that it should have occurred to me so early in my
artistic experience – that dancing does not have its source
necessarily in music, as was Dalcroze's theory. If one burns
to dance the movement bursts out spontaneously – a natural
reflex in a dancing nature. I have always loved pure movement, and I still do. That by no means prevents me enjoying movement with music. I love that passionately too.
Dalcroze was horrified and considered my thought an absolute
heresy; so I did not pursue it then. I dropped it and submitted
to him and his improvisations. I produced a few dances. He
would choose the music and I devised the dances, for instance
there was a Dance of Warriors for sixteen men, which I
arranged for a great public performance (and which we had to
encore). Now I think of it, it was a blatant imitation of
Isadora's *Danse des Scythes*. But I was not allowed to call it
ballet.

The next year Dalcroze accepted a long-standing offer
from two Germans, the brothers Dohrn, to move his school to
Hellerau, a garden city which was just being built outside

Dresden. The architect, von Tessenov, built a magnificent Institute for him with many studios. It had one big central hall designed by the great Adolphe Appia, who had completely revolutionised stage décor and lighting and, incidentally, considerably influenced Gordon Craig. There were also adjoining houses for the teaching staff as well as a big dining-hall. It was real luxury after the cramped quarters in Geneva, and the enthusiasm of the Dohrn management was most heartening after the distrust of the directing body of the Conservatoire of Geneva, who then, of course, began to see Dalcroze in a new light. (After the war they built him an Institute to replace the one in Hellerau.)

The other day I had a letter from a friend who had been at Dalcroze's school with me. She had found an old timetable of the lessons at Dresden and Hellerau and noticed that I was listed as giving seven lessons a week of *Turnen*, and she was very curious to know what sort of exercises *Turnen* could be? Was it a special method or a particular system?

Turnen is just the ordinary German word for gymnastic exercises, and I gave my classes that name because I knew I could not call them ballet, for ballet was anathema to Dalcroze. Of course what I actually taught my pupils was founded on ballet, because it was the only system I knew, but done barefoot and in Isadora's style.

In 1911 Dalcroze was invited to give lecture-demonstrations in Russia, and he took six pupils, of whom I was one, to illustrate them. The invitation came via Prince Serge Volkonsky, who had once been the Director of the Maryinsky. He was now a staunch supporter of Dalcroze. He was an immensely cultured man who had always been very interested in movement and rhythm. During his short directorate at the Maryinsky he had brought in many reforms and had invited Diaghilev to work with him there. But Diaghilev, with his very advanced views, very quickly got the authorities against him and after a year or two he was dismissed. Volkonsky did not stay very long either, because of his Western sympathies in art.

The long journey to St Petersburg passed gaily, with Dalcroze at his most entertaining. We arrived on a freezing cold day, with the temperature well below zero, and longing for a hot bath. We were led to a *bania* – a steam bath – to the amazement of the Swiss girls, though I had known it in Warsaw and Moscow. A huge, fat, naked woman, wearing nothing but a brass cross, received us at the entrance and proceeded to give us the full treatment which consisted of rubbing, scrubbing and whipping with birch twigs. We alternately cried and laughed at the harshness of the experience and the imperturbable naked lady ministering to us.

In St Petersburg we appeared at the Mikhailovsky Theatre, the Smolny Institute for Young Ladies of the Nobility and at the Conservatoire. As the Dowager Empress was the Patroness of the Smolny, we were given orders to wear a more modest attire than our black bathing-costumes. So we had instead a jersey, short pleated skirts and long opera stockings reaching right up to short knickers – all in black. We laughed to tears at all this paraphernalia, as we were dressing for the performance, with the result that when we were called on the stage at the Mikhailovsky, I forgot an essential garment. The first exercise we did was called *L'éveil au rythme*, which started off with us lying on the floor in a circle facing outward, so as not to see each other. At first Dalcroze played some vague dreamy music in which gradually the rhythm became more clear. At a certain point we began to beat out the rhythm with the hand only, then with the arm, then on the crescendo we had to raise ourselves on one knee and finally on the tonic chord we got to our feet and started marching victoriously. As we performed every action absolutely simultaneously, without looking at each other, because we reacted to the music completely identically, it always produced a great impression. But this time, just as I raised myself a little from

the floor I felt a fatal draught. A nightmare, I thought. But
no, it was a ghastly reality. I was right in front of the circle,
the others were already rising. There was nothing for it but
to crawl out ignominiously. As I writhed by the piano, Dalcroze whispered in a fury: 'Where are you off to?'

I reappeared in a few seconds, secure and happy. But forever
after he teased me whenever he could with: 'Got your knickers
on?'

The performances were received enthusiastically. We were
entertained in gorgeous palaces and taken for rides in sleighs
round the city, which was a revelation to the five girls and to
me enchanting as ever. At the house of some relations of
Volkonsky they had Rachmaninov to play after supper. Before
leaving we were each presented with a pendant from the
Dowager Empress. Alas, we did not value jewellery at the
time. I gave my aquamarine away, I cannot even remember to
whom.

In Moscow we performed at the Salle des Nobles, the
Conservatoire and, joy of joys, at the Moscow Arts Theatre.
To meet in person, and, what is more, to be treated as friends
by people like Stanislavsky, Kachalov and Olga Knipper
(Chekhov's wife, whom I met again in Moscow in 1934) was
more than we ever could hope for, or deserved. Stanislavsky
gave us a box to watch from on our free nights. We saw an
unforgettable *Uncle Vanya* (Kachalov in the title part) with
Stanislavsky as Astrov and Knipper as Elena; and also Gordon
Craig's production of *Hamlet* played by Kachalov, by far the
best Hamlet I have ever seen – and I try to see them all.

On our return from Russia we appeared in Leipzig, Hamburg and Frankfurt, and settled again to work at Hellerau.
In Hamburg I ate oysters for the first time, two dozen, with
nothing to follow – the best dinner I ever had.

One day our class was visited by Diaghilev and Nijinsky.
We had not been warned about their visit, as classical ballet
at that time was not one of our interests, and anyhow we often

had very distinguished visitors who came to watch our work. Diaghilev was a tall portly man with black hair which had a white streak above the right temple, and he looked leisurely and aristocratic. Nijinsky was a very small man with a pale complexion, fair sleek hair and light brown eyes slit slightly upward. Both were dressed very elegantly. They watched several classes and then had a conference with Dalcroze.

The next day, to my utter amazement, Dalcroze told me that Diaghilev wished to see me with a view to engaging me to join his company for special work. Though I was still in my anti-ballet, pro-Isadora phase, the prospect excited me immensely.

Diaghilev invited me to Berlin to watch a performance of his company with him, and afterwards at supper we discussed what shape my work might take. He listened politely, even sympathetically, to my stupid prejudiced criticism. I said I thought that the procession in *Cléopâtre* should have corresponded more exactly to the rhythm of the music, which was how Dalcroze would have done it. I know now that the great Fokine was absolutely right in his looser treatment of that passage. Diaghilev, however, did not defend him – they had fallen out by that time – and said:

'Yes, they walk like cooks – we must improve that.' (As though I was ever capable of improving on Fokine!)

L'Après-Midi d'un Faune was also in the programme. Here, the discrepancy between the impressionistic music of Debussy and Nijinsky's absolute austerity of style quite shocked me at the time. *Carnaval*, which came afterwards, enchanted me. I readily accepted Diaghilev's invitation to join the company, to acquaint them with Dalcroze's method, to help Nijinsky in applying it in the production of Stravinsky's *Sacre du Printemps* and to dance in ballets for which I was suitable.

I JOINED the company in Budapest, and was told by Serge Grigoriev, that incomparable *régisseur*, to watch rehearsals for a few days before starting my work. I was very impressed by his way of taking a rehearsal – his deep understanding of the choreography in all its details, his patient and lucid explanations to every artist. He knew the whole repertoire, having been the *régisseur* responsible for every point of the productions since the very beginning and remaining with Diaghilev for the whole twenty years of his reign. He described all this in his admirable book *The Diaghilev Ballet 1909–1929* which has since become a classic.

It proved impossible to find time for special classes in rhythm with the schedule already full of other vital work: a hard class every morning with Maestro Cecchetti, followed by rehearsals till lunch and after, and then a performance in the evening. So Grigoriev thought it more expedient for me to work with each artist individually in studying their parts in *Sacre du Printemps*, in which I was also to dance myself. Before the rehearsals of this ballet were started Diaghilev addressed the whole company explaining to them the theme of the ballet and enjoining them to reproduce faithfully the movements Nijinsky was going to compose. He knew full well that they were not looking forward to this, as they heartily detested the very stylised movements of his first ballet *L'Après-Midi d'un Faune*, which they considered the denial of their classical technique. In this they were quite wrong, as Nijinsky needed the best *classically* trained dancers to obtain his own precise style.

The work proceeded so slowly that Diaghilev decided on a long period of rehearsals in Monte Carlo without performances. We practically lived in the theatre. Some of the dancers snatched odd moments to gamble in the Casino. The boys were always asking for an advance on their wages to go and lose it there. I only went once, and had a most uncanny impression of the gamblers staring intently at the table. I had heard the stories of people coming out of the Casino and committing suicide in the garden next door. I was terrified and fled, just as I was later to flee from a bullfight the moment that the bull entered the ring.

There were lots of English in Monte Carlo at that time, and in many restaurants the menu had translations, sometimes quite hilarious. I saw one during a great fête, all printed in gold:

'A midi: Déjeuner de Gala suivi de Grande Bataille de fleurs! – Gala Luncheon followed by a Great Battle of flowers.

'A minuit: Souper de Gala suivi d'un Grand Defilé des mannequins. – At midnight, Gala Supper followed by a Grand Defiling of Mannequins.'

I had been put very quickly *au courant* of Diaghilev's relations with Nijinsky, and could not but share their admiration for each other. I once sat with Diaghilev in the stalls at a rehearsal of *Narcisse*.

He said, almost under his breath, 'What beauty!' and turning to me, 'Isn't he at his most perfect in this?'

'What about *Spectre*?'

'Of course, of course.'

'What about *Sylphides*? . . .'

And so we went on, all through Nijinsky's repertoire.

Every day, after the general rehearsal, I had to stay for an hour or two and listen with Nijinsky to the score of *Sacre*. He then sketched out the movements for the next rehearsal. The rhythms were very difficult, and I had to study the rhythm with each artist individually. They soon nicknamed me 'Rythmichka'. There was no melody to hold on to – so the only way to learn it was to count the bars all the time. The movements in themselves were simple, and so was the floor pattern. But the basic position was difficult to sustain in movement, and the mastering of that rhythm almost impossible.

Diaghilev had a valet called Vassily Zhukov. They suspected in the company that he was so devoted to Diaghilev because he had been saved by him in Russia from a heavy sentence for some serious crime – they said it was rape in particularly sordid circumstances. Anyway Diaghilev got him off, and now his devotion embraced Nijinsky too, because he knew how precious he was to Diaghilev.

Always when in *Spectre de la Rose* Nijinsky did his last spectacular jump out of the window, Vassily would lay him down on a mattress on the floor and mop his brow and face. Nijinsky gasped and kept saying, 'Vady, vady' (water, water), and Vassily would let him have a sip of warm water, but take it away at once before he drank too much. I saw Diaghilev sometimes there too, most solicitous, as though Nijinsky was in serious danger.

When Diaghilev went to Russia to try and arrange a season for the company at the Narodny Dom (the Theatre of the People) – which came to nothing because the theatre was burnt down before we could go there – he left behind his faithful Vassily. We couldn't rehearse for twenty minutes without Vassily coming in and saying, 'Vaslav Fomich, we'd better open the window. It's very stuffy in here, it's not good for you.' Then he would go out. But half an hour later he would come in again and say, 'Vaslav Fomich, you know, I think it's rather draughty now, we'd better shut the window.'

He was really spying on us, though there was nothing to spy on, because Nijinsky didn't take the slightest notice of me as a woman. It never occurred to him, it never occurred to me. We were only discussing the work in hand.

After rehearsals we sometimes used to go to Chez Pasquier to drink chocolate and eat gateaux, and talk about our work. We never made arrangements to go out together, but it so happened that we were mostly both ready at the same time. One day I was ready to go before he was, and not wishing to wait for him too obviously, I just went to Pasquier by myself. I had been sitting there a few minutes, when in walked Nijinsky, looking as pale as a ghost.

'What on earth is the matter?' I asked.

'I very nearly killed a man.'

'How can you say such a thing?' Anyhow, who was it?'

'A blackguard, a brigand, who has prevented Bronia from dancing *Jeux* and *Sacre*.'

'But who is he?'

'Kochetovsky!'

Bronia was Nijinsky's sister, very closely akin to him in temperament, and she was one of the best dancers in the company. Kochetovsky was her husband. Naturally I began to reason with Nijinsky and said it must all have been a misunderstanding and that Bronia would not lightly give up her role in *Sacre* and *Jeux*. Moreover, I reminded him that the previous year Bronia walked out because, although it was her turn to dance the ballerina in *Petrushka* (she shared it with Karsavina) on the opening night in London, Diaghilev had bowed to Sir Joseph Beecham's insistence that Karsavina should appear. Bronia and her husband did not return for a couple of days only – it was all patched up by then.

But Nijinsky kept repeating that through that blackguard's fault she would not create these roles conceived by him with Bronia in mind.

The next day came the official announcement that Bronia was pregnant and would not dance in our Paris and London seasons. And *this* was her husband's great crime.

When Stravinsky first came to one of our rehearsals and heard the way his music was being played, he blazed up, pushed aside the fat German pianist, nicknamed 'Kolossal' by Diaghilev, and proceeded to play twice as fast as we had been doing it, and twice as fast as we could possibly dance. He stamped his feet on the floor and banged his fist on the piano and sang and shouted, all to give us an impression of the rhythms of the music and the colour of the orchestra.

It was an epic quarrel between Stravinsky and Nijinsky. But somehow or other Diaghilev managed to calm them down.

Many years later, when the Bolshoi Ballet made its second visit to this country in 1969, their chief choreographer, Gregorovich (whose superb *Spartacus* showed how much one can still say in purely classical language if one burns with passion) told me that though Stravinsky had bitterly disapproved of Nijinsky's version in 1913, he had since admitted that it was by far the best rendering of his *Sacre*.

In 1913 Stravinsky's music came as a shock, especially by comparison with the rest of the repertoire – Chopin, Schumann and Borodin, with their lovely and easily remembered tunes. It is true that the company had already danced two ballets of Stravinsky: *The Firebird* and *Petrushka*, but these were infinitely easier to memorise with their clear melodies, perfectly translated by Fokine into wonderful dances. The more I saw them the more I was enchanted by their real musicality, in comparison with Dalcroze's purely theoretical translation of the music.

Soon I joined Cecchetti's classes and recognised the teaching of my first master Slowacki. But now I wore proper ballet shoes and did a hard class every day as well as a practice on my own. In this Nijinsky helped me quite often by explaining details to me entirely in his own way. Explaining is the wrong word when applied to Nijinsky. He spoke very little, and words did not come easily to him, which is why the rehearsing of his ballets always took so long. But he demonstrated the details of the movement so clearly and perfectly that it left no doubt as to the way it had to be done. He had such a high arch and such strength and suppleness of foot that the sole of one foot could clasp the back of the ankle of the other as though it were a hand (in the position *sur le cou de pied*). In addition to the class every morning which we all did, he used to do all the exercises again, this time partly made up, in preparation for the performance. Of course, I never failed to watch that.

One is often asked whether his jump was really as high as it is always described. To that I answer: 'I don't know how far from the ground it was, but I know it was near the stars.' Who would watch the floor when he danced? He transported you at once into higher spheres with the sheer ecstacy of his flight.

The most absurd theories were put forward about his anatomy. People said that the bones in his feet were like a bird's – as though a bird flew because of its feet! But, in fact, he *did* have an exceptionally long Achilles tendon which allowed him with his heels firmly on the ground and the back upright to bend the knees to the utmost before taking a spring, and he had powerful thighs. As to his famous poising in the air, he indeed created the illusion of it by the ecstasy of his expression at the apex of the leap, so that *this* unique moment penetrated into every spectator's consciousness, and seemed to last. His landing, from whatever height he jumped, was like a cat's. He had that unique touch of the foot on the ground which can only be compared to the pianist's touch of the fingers on the keys. It was as subtle and as varied.

And then there was his unique interpretation. He wafted the perfume of the rose in *Spectre de la Rose*; he was the very spirit of Chopin in *Les Sylphides*; he looked like a Hamlet in *Giselle*; his Petrushka broke your heart with his sorrow, and his Faune had the real breath of antiquity.

As to his choreography, I would not hesitate to affirm that it was he, more than anyone else, who revolutionised the classical ballet and was fifty years ahead of his time. Fokine was a logical development of Petipa, but Nijinsky introduced completely new principles. He produced three ballets in all: *l'Après-Midi d'un Faune, Jeux* and *Sacre du Printemps*. For each of them he established a basic position strictly adhered to all through the ballet. For *Faune* he took his inspiration from Greek vases and bas-reliefs. The body was facing front while the head and feet were always seen in profile. The deportment had to be classical, yet the head had independent movements not connected with deportment in the classical vocabulary, and so had the arms. It was an orchestration of the body, with each part playing a totally different melody. There was nothing you could do automatically. The walking was all done on one line parallel to the footlights, the whole foot on the ground. It was an incredibly difficult position to achieve, let alone use in walking, or changing direction, or combining with highly stylised arm movements. He did not explain why he wanted them thus, but he showed again and again the way they had to be done until he obtained a perfect copy of his own movement. His method of creation was diametrically opposed to Fokine's. Fokine always took the dancers into his confidence and allowed them, even encouraged them, to participate in the creation of a character. Not so Nijinsky. When once I was extolling the virtues of *Petrushka* to him, saying it was Fokine's masterpiece, he said that it *was* so, as far as the three main characters went, but the crowd was treated too loosely, and everybody did what they wanted within the space indicated to them. Nijinsky on the contrary did not allow the slightest freedom of movement or gesture and exacted only a perfect copy. No wonder it took some hundred and twenty rehearsals for *l'Après-midi d'un Faune*, lasting about ten minutes, to be achieved as he wished, since not a single move-ment could be done spontaneously, each limb having to be studied separately. He required a perfect ballet technique and then broke it down consciously to his own purpose – and then it proved a masterpiece. Each nymph looked a goddess. Although they were incapable of understanding Nijinsky's intentions, the mere fact of faithfully copying his unique movements gave them the requisite style. He told them: no expression in the face, you must just be as though asleep with your eyes open – like statues.

Once when a new girl had to learn Nijinsky's sister's part, in which the Nymph suddenly sees the Faune, turns away and walks off – he said to her: 'Why do you look so frightened?'

She said she thought she was meant to be. Thereupon, quite in a rage, he said that the movement he gave her was all that was required of her, he was not interested in her personal feelings. And how right Nijinsky was for his particular choreography! It acquired an impersonal, remote character – just like the paintings on Greek vases or bas-reliefs – not that he ever attempted to copy any particular poses from these, but created them by the profoundest penetration into their very spirit. The walking was done not strictly to the music, but rather loosely as though walking 'through' the music.

I was talking to him about Nelidova, the dancer who had been brought from Moscow to do the picturesque Ida Rubinstein parts in the repertoire and who, as the Chief Nymph, looked like Pallas Athene (after a hundred and twenty rehearsals, mind you). I said I imagined she would be deeply grateful to him for having presented her in such a marvellous creation.

He smiled ironically and retorted: 'She, grateful? Never! She would prefer me to write a Spanish dance for her with a rose behind her ear and a carnation in her teeth to show off her hot temperament!'

How right he was, for she was incapable of appreciating his genius, and only blind obedience to his orders transformed her from a silly – though talented – woman into a goddess. The photographs between pages 80 and 81 should give a good idea of the character of the poses.

I have a film of *Faune* made when the ballet was reproduced for my company in 1931 by Woizikowsky, who had danced the *Faune* in the last year of Diaghilev and remembered it well. Nijinsky created a special walk for the faune: short sudden steps with the second foot coming up quickly to the first one. There was only one powerful leap – he called it the goat's leap.

The shred of a plot could just be guessed, as it was told in those very abstract movements with the face totally impassive. The nymphs come to bathe unaware that they are watched by the faun, who is reclining on a rock. The chief nymph takes off one after the other her two veils, which the nymphs carry away, and remains in a little golden shirt with a thin scarf in her hands. He tries to follow her, and for one long moment while she is kneeling he stands beside her with his right arm linked through her left. She withdraws her arm and slips away, leaving her veil. The nymphs reappear to mock him and run away. He picks up the veil and it represents to him the nymph herself. He carries it off to his rock, lays it out on the ground and presses himself full length to it.

The half-man, half-goat of his faun, the unknowing bathing nymphs, the heat of that somnolent afternoon – all created a world of its own, and Debussy's impressionistic music receded completely into the background before this epic evocation of Greek antiquity.

It was the painter Roerich who first suggested the subject of *Sacre du Printemps*. He then worked on the theme with Diaghilev, Stravinsky and Nijinsky. It was to be prehistoric Russia and represent the rites of spring. Stravinsky had finished his magnificent score by 1912, and we started the rehearsals with the company that same year.

Nijinsky again first of all established the basic position: feet very turned in, knees slightly bent, arms held in reverse of the classical position, a primitive, prehistoric posture. The steps were very simple: walking smoothly or stamping, jumps mostly off both feet, landing heavily. There was only one a little more complicated dance for the maidens in the first scene.

It was mostly done in groups, and each group has its own precise rhythm to follow. In the dance (if one can call it that) of the Wisest Elder, he walked two steps against every three steps of the ensemble. In the second scene the dance of the sacrifice of the Chosen Virgin was powerful and deeply moving. I watched Nijinsky again and again teaching it to Maria Piltz. Her reproduction was very pale by comparison with his ecstatic performance, which was the greatest tragic dance I have ever seen.

The first night of that ballet was the most astonishing event. Already the music of *Petrushka* had provoked the absolute hatred of the Vienna orchestra when we danced there in 1912. At rehearsal they threw down their bows in fury and called it 'Schweinerei'. Diaghilev went down into the pit and argued with them for quite a while before they consented to play – and then they sabotaged it.

And now in Paris in 1913 at the first sounds of the music, shouts and hissing started in the audience, and it was very difficult for us on the stage to hear the music, the more so as part of the audience began to applaud in an attempt to drown the hissing. We all desperately tried to keep time without being able to hear the rhythm clearly. In the wings Nijinsky counted the bars to guide us. Pierre Monteux conducted undeterred, Diaghilev having told him to continue to play at all costs.

But after the interlude things became even worse, and during the sacrificial dance real pandemonium broke out. That scene began with Maria Piltz, the Chosen Virgin, standing on the spot trembling for many bars, her folded hands under her right cheek, her feet turned in, a truly prehistoric and beautiful pose. But to the audience of the time it appeared ugly and comical.

A shout went up in the gallery:

'Un docteur!'

Somebody else shouted louder:

14. At Geneva: happy dancing

15. In front of Dalcroze's institute at Hellerau in 1910. I am second from the left

16. Peter Scott: one of my first eurhythmics pupils

17. A picnic with Dalcroze at Kew Gardens. On the right Paulet Thévenaz. I am in the back row in the chic black hat

18. Diaghilev in his early days at St Petersburg

19. Diaghilev

'Un dentiste!'

Then someone else screamed:

'Deux dentistes!'

And so it went on. One elegant lady leaned out of her box and slapped a man who was clapping. But the performance went on to the end.

And yet now there is no doubt that, musically and choreographically, a masterpiece had been created that night. The only ballet that could compare with it in power was Bronislava Nijinska's *Les Noces*, created in 1923. She, like her brother, produced a truly epic ballet – so far unexcelled anywhere.

After the first night of *Sacre* was over, we were all far too excited to think of going home to bed. A great gang of us – I can't remember who we all were – went off and had a great supper at a restaurant called the Reine Pédauque. When we had finished supper, we all went in fiacres to the Bois de Boulogne and walked, and ran about, and played games on the grass and among the trees for most of the night. At about two o'clock in the morning we went to the restaurant at the Pré Catelan in the Bois de Boulogne and had yet another supper. And so went on eating and drinking and whiling away time in the park until morning. We finished the night by having breakfast at a dairy in Marie Antoinette's Petit Palais.

When it was all over I did not go home to my aunt's because there were no baths there, and above all things I wanted a bath. I went to Edmée's, and there I had a hot bath and a cold shower. After that I felt I was all set up to face a lesson with Cecchetti. So off I went to the Maestro's class, but when I got there I found that I was so tired and dazed that I could not stand on two legs, let alone one. Cecchetti shouted at me – and with good reason. I suppose there must have been some others in the class who were in the same state, but I was so giddy that even if I had noticed them at the time I certainly do not remember them.

During the lesson I was offered a ticket to go to the opera

with Fraülein von Senf and her parents that night and hear Chaliapine in *Boris Godounov* presented by Diaghilev, which had opened in Paris only a week before. I had not seen it yet because of the rehearsals of *Sacre*. Of course I went, although by now I was quite exhausted. But when I sat in the box with the von Senfs, it seemed to me that Chaliapine singing Moussorgsky's music was no better than the singers one heard out of the window singing for sous. The von Senfs were horrified by me, but I remained obstinate, and even had the temerity to argue that Chaliapine's glory was overrated and that Moussorgsky's music was dull. I really was *non compos*.

I suppose it cannot have been long before I saw Chaliapine on the stage again, for I went to all the operas, and realised how wrong I had been, and that his performance in Benois's setting and Sanine's production was operatic art at its greatest.

At one of the performances the chorus refused to go on until Diaghilev would pay them – there had already been some disputes about pay. But Chaliapine was resolved not to let the public down, and so he came on the stage after the interval. I saw him sitting on his throne in the magnificent coronation robes, when the chorus rushed on appropriately dressed for that scene as the Moscow rabble and someone struck him. It was like a scene in a great tragedy where one saw real majesty attacked by baseness.

But when I first saw the opera I was blind to his majesty, such was the strange indirect effect of the excitement over *Sacre*, which has remained with me to this day. I also have other records of *Sacre*. After Nijinsky had left Diaghilev and I was already living in London, I wrote to Stravinsky and said that while I still remembered everything that Nijinsky said during the rehearsals of *Sacre* I should very much like to write it down on the score. But I hadn't got one. Could he please send me a piano score?

He promptly sent me his own arrangement of the music of *Sacre* for four hands, and I carefully wrote down above the

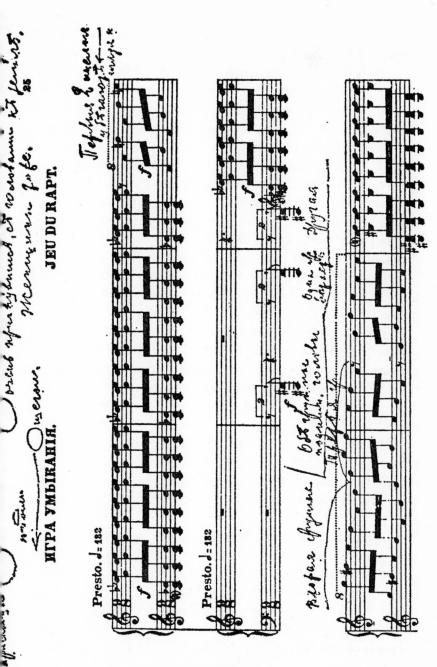

My notes in Russian on the score of *Sacre* give an idea of the phrases Nijinsky used to describe the dancers. The circles at the top represent the various groups, 'fine fellows', 'lads', 'wenches', and on the right 'a big group of fellows sit on the ground, very bent, peering into the earth. The women do the same.'

music the actual words that Nijinsky spoke during rehearsals. It was not a choreographic record, naming the steps, but Nijinsky's comments and enlightening remarks.

I couldn't play a score for four hands, so I put it away and forgot all about it until some fifty years later, when Nigel Gosling came to see me. We were talking about Stravinsky, and I suddenly remembered that I had a score of *Sacre*.

So I found it and showed it to Nigel. He looked at the music and then said, 'What are these things written here?'

There, written in the old Russian orthography – the Soviets have since suppressed various unnecessary letters – were all the remarks Nijinsky made, just as he had said them in Russian. They would not enable one to reproduce the ballet. But they do help one to feel the personality of Nijinsky and to see exactly how he spoke and the rather special language he used during the rehearsals.

Nijinsky's next ballet was *Jeux*, to music by Debussy. (It was actually performed just before *Sacre*, but it is less important.) Here, too, he proved a revolutionary, for he was the first choreographer to bring a contemporary situation into ballet, and the three protagonists wore sports clothes of the day.

Although the ballet started with a huge tennis ball flying across the stage from the wings and Nijinsky with a racket in his hand leaping on, there was no further reference to tennis after that but a sort of flirtation between the three players. The audience looked in blank amazement at the three stars: Karsavina, Nijinsky and Schollar doing what appeared to them quite childish movements. They had of course expected great feats of virtuosity. But the movements, seemingly simple, were, as in all Nijinsky's choreography, very difficult to carry out – that is why he insisted on having the two ballerinas.

It is probable that at some moment Nijinsky had the idea of doing *Jeux* on full point. He brought one day a pair of point shoes (ballet shoes with reinforced ends to the toes) and tried some exercises at the barre. I watched amazed, but he did not volunteer any explanation. After a while he took the shoes off. Probably if he had not found it so hard he would have made the two ballerinas dance on full point too, and made them much happier, as they heartily detested doing his steps on half point.

One evening, as we were coming out of a late rehearsal, Nijinsky pointed upwards to the electrically lit-up trees and said, 'This is the lighting I want for *Jeux*.'

'What! For a game of tennis?' I asked amazed.

He smiled enigmatically, signifying an indefinite 'Yes'.

Karsavina, who had created all the great roles in Fokine's ballets, once asked Nijinsky during a rehearsal to elucidate some point. He flew into a rage and shouted that she had 'a ballerina mentality' – the most ludicrous accusation, for she had the finest intelligence, culture and generosity of nature, added to her unique artistry and beauty. She naturally walked out.

Thereupon Diaghilev, furious, shouted: 'How dare you insult that great artist, you are nothing but a guttersnipe to her, go at once and beg her to forgive you!'

Jeux was to open the 1913 season at the inauguration of the Théâtre des Champs-Elysées. The theatre was not quite finished when we came to rehearse there, and we were frequently interrupted by workmen crossing the room to go on the roof. This exasperated Nijinsky, who was in a hurry to finish his ballet, and he screamed that next time someone crossed the room he would kill him. He indeed seized a chair to hurl it at the man, but of course was stopped in time. I wonder if this, like his earlier outburst against Kochetovsky, was a sign of the beginning of his illness?

The costumes for *Jeux* were designed by Bakst, and at the dress-rehearsal Nijinsky appeared for the first time in his costume so that we could see it. I was sitting near Diaghilev in the dress circle; and rather nearer the stage on the left, was Bakst. Nijinsky leapt on to the stage wearing Bakst's idea of the sports costume for a tennis-player: hideous long shorts almost down to his knees and making his legs look very thick (we were used to tights which softened the line), thick socks half way up his legs, and to top it all . . . a red wig.

Diaghilev was appalled, and started shouting at Bakst, 'He can't go on like that, Lyovushka!'

And Bakst shouted back, 'How dare you say he can't go on, Seryozha? It's designed, and it's made, and it's going to go on.'

And so they went on slanging one another; yet, funnily enough, however angry they got, they still called each other by their pet names.

'I won't alter a stitch, Seryozha,' yelled Bakst.

'All right, Lyovushka,' replied Diaghilev. 'But they are not going to appear in these costumes.'

So he sent the women – I forget what Bakst designed for them originally – to Paquin, the great couturier, who made them very pretty white skirts and jerseys. And for Nijinsky, Diaghilev simply said that he should wear his own hair, a white shirt with the sleeves rolled up, and trousers caught at the ankles and leaving the foot free, such as were used at the Maryinsky for classes and rehearsals, only made of white cloth instead of black. At that time the men did not wear tights, but trousers, both for classes and rehearsals. Only the girls wore tights with their tutus.

From Paris we went to London. This was not the first time I came to England. The company had visited the country in 1912, and I had been eager, on that first occasion, to see London. As our train approached the station, I looked out of the window and said to Nijinsky, 'Where is London?'

'This *is* London,' he replied.

'Where?' I said again, for I could see nothing.

'Here.'

We had arrived in the middle of a pea-soup fog.

Even when it cleared, London made little impression on me. I am not a real traveller who looks for new places. When I walk I don't (unfortunately) observe what is around me. I usually think either about my work, or very likely am saying to myself some newly learnt poem. I know that nobody will believe me when I say that it took me *three* weeks to learn the shortest way to the Mercury – which is about five minutes away from my house! I can go to the same city ten times and still not find my way to the theatre. They always have to send somebody to take me to the stage door. My husband summed it up very aptly when he said to me: 'You have the unerring sense of the wrong direction.'

On that first visit to London, somebody in the company recommended me a hotel in Gerrard Street – of all places. The receptionist was forbidding, and the people in the lounge looked to me like bandits, so that I was quite frightened. Next morning, in absolute distress, I went to see Mr Ingham and his wife, an elderly couple whom I had known at Dalcroze's school and had afterwards become very friendly with, and they recommended some good rooms to me.

On my second visit the Inghams recommended me to a boarding-house in Lamb's Conduit Street. The name puzzled me very much, for I thought it referred to the conduct of lambs, and wondered what that could be. I had no time to see any more of London, except to learn my way from Lamb's Conduit Street to the Aldwych Theatre, which Diaghilev had taken for the rehearsals of *Sacre du Printemps*.

But neither *Sacre* nor *Jeux* made any greater impression in London than they had in Paris, and they were never seen again with Nijinsky's choreography.

At the end of the London season in the summer of 1913 we went to South America. None of Nijinsky's works were taken, only the easiest ballets of the repertoire.

Diaghilev did not want to cross the ocean – apparently a gypsy had warned him against death by water. Be that as it may, it was his *not* coming on that voyage that proved a disaster to him.

I had made friends in Paris with a young Hungarian, Romola de Pulsky, who had had some lessons with Maestro Cecchetti. She was very beautiful, elegant and cultivated, and I was delighted to hear that she was coming with the company to South America. I used to love watching Romola having her glorious ash-blond hair (natural!) brushed by her Hungarian maid, while we had endless talks about Nijinsky, whom we both adored.

But my chief joy on the boat were conversations with Nijinsky himself. He lent me his volumes of *Mir Iskustva* (*The World of Art*), a periodical edited by Diaghilev, and we talked about the various articles in it, specially Merejkovsky's about Tolstoy and Dostoevsky, for whom we shared the same enthusiasm. A memorable phrase of Diaghilev's in one of his own articles was 'Beauty in art is feeling expressed in images.' How illuminating!

Although Nijinsky was a man of few words, he could express his thoughts clearly, though with difficulty, and I was struck by his knowledge and feeling for literature. He also had wit, and often made me laugh with his unexpected observations. For instance, I once asked him what sort of man was one of our staff who happened just to be passing by. 'Oh him? He writes little short stories on the sly for *Kurjer Warszawski*. The last one is called: "Her little pinny".' And it really described the whole of that man. This man was very friendly with one of the handsomest girls in the *corps de ballet*, Jozefina Kowalewska, who had been a mistress of the Aga Khan. The Aga Khan was always begging Diaghilev to give her some distinctive role outside the *corps de ballet*. But the only concessions he would make was to allow her to wear a black dress inside a circle of the *corps de ballet* in white. This was in *Cléopâtre*.

Kowalewska was a great fool and totally ignorant of everything. She always made mistakes in her long Christian name and surname when signing her photographs. One day, as a joke, someone rushed into her dressing-room and exclaimed, 'Have you heard the news? Napoleon is dead!'

'Oh,' she cried, clapping a hand to her face. 'How dreadful for Paris!'

This amused the company so much that we insisted on a repeat performance. Once again someone rushed into her dressing-room, but this time he said: 'Have you heard the news? Napoleon's brother is dead!'

And sure enough Kowalewska clapped her hand to her face and said, 'Oh, how dreadful for Paris!'

Our journey lasted twenty-two days. The principals travelled first class, but we, the *corps de ballet*, went second. Romola was in the first class, presumably at her own expense.

Nobody did any practice, it was too hot. We just lay about in deck-chairs, or sauntered slowly up and down the decks. I was often invited by my great friends, the Rhené-Bâtons (our conductor and his wife), to visit them on the first class deck; and it was then that I could meet Nijinsky and have our long strolls and talks. Once some deck game was being played, I forget what, but several of us were sitting in a semi-circle watching it, with the men standing behind. I suddenly felt faint (we were nearing the tropics) and was about to fall, when two strong arms lifted me up and out of the circle. As I opened my eyes – oh, joy of joys – it was Nijinsky. A second of bliss. This was the only *pas de deux* I ever did with Nijinsky.

As we were approaching Rio de Janeiro I saw Nijinsky in a group with the Rhené-Bâtons and Romola. He was giving her a light for her cigarette – it seemed such a courteous, elegant gesture (though I myself always loathed smoking) and so unexpected. Another time, as Rhené Bâton shook her hand rather vigorously in greeting, Nijinsky, quite alarmed, called out, 'Pas casser! Pas casser!' in his childish French. It is true that she had very delicate wrists.

But all this did not worry me at all – it seemed to me so slight. In the last week Nijinsky told me, almost as a joke, that he was in love with Romola. I asked what language he talked to her, for she had no Russian and his French was so primitive.

'Oh, she understands everything,' he said, smiling wistfully.

I did not believe it was serious. We all knew he was Diaghilev's lover. But when we arrived in Rio we spent a whole day on shore, he alone with Romola and the rest of us in groups. On our return Madame Bâton came into my cabin and told me joyously that Nijinsky and Romola had announced their engagement. This gave me a terrible shock – I suddenly realised that I was hopelessly in love with him, and had been for a long time. I bent down over my cabin trunk and pretended to rummage in it so as to hide my hot tears. Later in the evening I went out on the empty deck and stood bending over the rail longing for the ocean to swallow me. And yet that very moment saved me from the bitter life of Romola, whom I so envied then. Eventually, as luck would have it, I was found on deck by my partner in *Schéhérazade*, a young man whom I always found a nuisance, and who could not have been more so than at that moment.

The wedding took place in Buenos Aires. Karsavina made the most graceful and enchanting speech – a speech that only she could make. Of all the women that I know on earth, she is the one who could never do a thing that was not full of grace, whether she was giving a speech or a lecture, joking with friends, or writing a book. She has a most remarkable and refined intelligence and her autobiography is a classic.

Bolm, on the other hand, made the most tactless speech, saying that of all the great leaps Nijinsky had ever made this was the most prodigious one: the jump from his former life into marriage!

I hardly ever saw Nijinsky after that till the end of the tour, except of course on the stage. On our return journey he and his wife kept to their cabin.

There are many theories nowadays about the sudden reversal of feelings in Nijinsky. Be that as it may, my personal tragedy had nothing to do with it at all.

On our way to South America we were constantly reminded about the danger of the 'white slave traffic' and warned not to talk to strangers. Yet no arrangements about our lodgings were made, and we trudged with our luggage in the sweltering heat. After some two hours I at last found a passable-looking place where the landlady spoke French. She was too amiable from the beginning, but I was so exhausted that I stayed there. At supper she told me of 'a gentleman who is very attracted by you'. He had changed boat as soon as he saw our company change, and he longed to meet me. I said that was impossible, I would only meet the people to whom I had letters of introduction. She assured me that he was very nice and generous and that last year he had taken a fancy to a singer and had given her a necklace and ear-rings and she had not given him anything – 'not even *that*'. She clicked her thumb-nail against her teeth.

Next day I was having my siesta in my locked room. There was a knock at the door.

'The gentleman is here and wishes to see you.'

'Please send him away.'

Half an hour later, another knock:

'The gentleman is waiting for you, and when he asks you what you like to drink, say champagne.'

'Go away.'

By now it was time to go for rehearsal, and, though I was frightened, I decided to go out. I was running downstairs from my second-floor room when the landlady caught me on the landing of the first floor and flung me into the drawing-room, where a hideous man – he seemed to me a monster – took me by the hand. I tore myself away and ran out of the *pension* and all the way to the rehearsal. I never went back; my luggage was collected and my bill paid by one of the boys of the company.

I went to a *pension* with the rest of the company. We had to go to rehearsals on a tram, which stopped at the bottom of a steep hill. Groups of young local men used to wait there to catch a glimpse of the dancers' ankles, though our dresses at the time nearly touched the ground. Once there was an odd incident on the way back to the *pension*. All my life I have never been able to drink real coffee, as it stimulates me too much and prevents me from sleeping, even if I take it in the morning. (Now I am able to have decaffeinated coffee – 'decapitated', as a friend of mine calls it.) Passing a café in Rio, I caught the fragrance of fresh Brazilian coffee roasting. Unable to resist it, I went in and had a cup, with devastating results. Jumping on to a fast-moving tram I arrived at our *pension*. I was late and my friends, who were worried about me, were waiting impatiently at the top of the outside steps. I reached them by climbing a wall that was bare apart from a few slim creepers. No one could stop me. I was positively drunk on that coffee, fearless and as agile as a monkey. Next day I couldn't believe that I had done it, but for the testimony of all the witnesses who had attempted in vain to stop me.

Cecchetti did not come on that tour and we had no regular lessons – it was too hot. Only Karsavina continued to practise every day (not on the boat, but in the towns), and in her kindness allowed me to work at the same time. I learnt a great deal watching her at close quarters, and from time to time she even gave me explanations and corrections. The tour would soon be over, and I had to think about the future. We had danced in four cities, Rio de Janeiro, Buenos Aires, Montevideo and São Paulo.

In my conversations with Nijinsky on the boat he had told me that my weak technique would hinder me all my life, unless I took time off straight away and studied seriously for a couple of years.

'Otherwise,' he said, 'you can never hope to blossom out as a dancer. Besides,' he added with remarkable vision, 'this is not the right company for you – you must find another type altogether.'

Ultimately he proved right and I founded my own company as a result.

I doubt if I would have had the courage to leave the company of my own accord, but when the South American tour was over I had no choice. Nijinsky's contract was not renewed after his marriage, and his ballets were not kept in the repertoire, and as I was supposed to be helping teach rhythm for his ballets, they did not renew mine either, and I left on our return to Paris.

But before I leave the subject of the Diaghilev Ballet I

should like to put down what I remember of my own part in the ballets in which I danced.

In *Swan Lake* I was one of the *corps de ballet*, and I had a thrilling moment when we stood in couples on both sides of the stage, and the Prince – Nijinsky – came scrutinising each face to find Odette. I was in the last row with another girl right at the back. There was a heavenly moment of waiting for him to approach, and then for one second he looked into my face before passing on.

In *Giselle* I was also in the *corps de ballet*.

In *Schéhérazade* I was one of the Shah's wives who cavorted with their Negro lovers when the Shah was away. There was Nijinsky with Zobeïde, the Shah's favourite wife, and a whole cohort of the rest of us. Fokine didn't give us any special movements for this scene. It was left to the dancers, in the way Nijinsky so much disapproved of. We were just given rugs and cushions scattered about the stage, and Fokine said, 'You rush there, and you embrace – you two on this cushion, and you two on that,' and so on.

Unfortunately the boy with whom I had to dance, the same one who found me weeping on deck when Nijinsky's engagement was announced, was after me, though I couldn't stand him, and he had free play on our cushion.

In *Thamar* I only remember that I was one of those with pill-box hats with a long veil underneath, very picturesque. It was a Caucasian costume.

In *Prince Igor*, I was one of the Polovtsian girls who wore many-coloured Russian boots. Fedorova, our principal character ballerina, was the chief Polovtsian, and one evening I was chatting with her in her dressing-room, when the cashier came in with a wad of notes – her salary. We had already been called on the stage, so he offered to come in later. But she took the packet and shoved it down her leg into her boot – and danced with even more fire than usual.

In *Cléopâtre* I was one of the Bacchantes, which was easy

for me, for it was the so-called Greek dancing of the time, and I danced barefoot – or as barefoot as was permitted by the conventions of the time. Actually we wore tights, but tights with separate toes to them, like gloves. They were extraordinarily difficult to put on because one always forgot which toe went into which 'finger', and one cannot control toes like fingers. Only later did Diaghilev's dancers appear with really bare feet.

In *Sacre* I was one of the Four with Hilda Bewicke, Poiré and Kokhlova (who later married Picasso). On the first night Nijinsky made us all up himself, using a very stylised make-up to go with the stylised and primitive movements he had devised. But after the first night we reverted to our ordinary make-up.

The last time I saw Nijinsky was in Paris in 1928. I had gone to the Paris Opéra to see the Diaghilev Company in a performance of *Petrushka*. Karsavina was dancing and so was Lifar. I noticed Diaghilev sitting in a box and recognised him at once; but I couldn't quite see who was with him, partly because it was a side box and I was in the centre, and also I don't think I would have recognised the face anyway.

After the performance was over I dashed back stage to Lifar's room to contratulate him. He had danced Petrushka magnificently, indeed at that time, under Diaghilev, he was a brilliant dancer.

As soon as I entered Lifar's dressing-room, he said, 'Have you seen Nijinsky?'

'Why? Where?' I replied.

'Serguey Pavlovich' (this was Diaghilev's name) 'has just taken him down to see him off. If you run very fast you'll see him.'

The back of the Opéra is an incredible maze, a labyrinth of stairs and passageways. But somehow I found my way and rushed along them until I found myself looking down from the top of the last flight of stairs. At the bottom I saw

Diaghilev holding Nijinsky's hand and leading him away. Then I saw that absolutely blank face, and I thought, 'No, I'm not going to try to talk to him or touch his hand.' It hurt me bitterly to see what had become of that marvellous human being.

In Paris I went at once to see dear old Madame Rat again to arrange lessons, and started working very hard straight away. Having studied with Cecchetti, I now knew how to take the best of what she had to teach me – and to leave the rest. After having seen at such close quarters how hard Nijinsky and Karsavina worked, I put all my heart into my classes. I also arranged a whole new programme of my own dances, and armed with Colette Willy's letter of introduction went to see the manager of the Théâtre Impérial in the Champs Elysées, who offered to present me there for two recitals. I had enthusiastic notices in *Le Temps* and *L'Intransigeant*, and I received at once many invitations to appear at private houses, sometimes well paid and almost always interesting.

Among the houses in which I danced, one of the most remarkable was the *salon* of Madeleine Lemaire, the very aged friend of Proust – though I did not meet him, alas. She was most amiable to me, and at one of her receptions Saint-Saëns played for me.

I made many interesting acquaintances and one life-long friendship, with Vera Donnet. She was a Russian, who had been married to a Swiss, and later to an Englishman, Harold Bowen. She was a woman of the highest intelligence and culture, as well as unique charm, and we forthwith began to meet every day and all day. She taught me elegance in dress, which I needed badly in the circles where I performed. Before that I had been terribly 'aesthetic' under the influence of Raymond Duncan. I was wild and had no manners. She tried to tame me, with little success, I fear. Her advice in art as well as in life was *law* to me – and I never ignored it.

20. Nijinsky in *Petrushka*

21. Nijinsky and his sister Bronislava
in *L'Après-Midi d'un Faune*

22. Nijinsky in *Le Spectre de la Rose*

23. Nelidova looking like Pallas
Athene in *Faune*

24. The maidens in *Le Sacre du Printemps*.
I am second from the left

25. On the boat to South
America, Kovalevska,
Rambert, Oblakova,
Pflanz

26, 27, 28, 29. In recital numbers

30. (*below*, *left*) Vera Donnet: my mentor in art

31, 32. The result of her lessons in chic

Diaghilev gave his last pre-war season in May 1914. I went to watch a rehearsal and noticed a beautiful youth with Byzantine eyes having a private lesson from Maestro Cecchetti. Diaghilev told me it was Massine.

'He is going to dance *La Légende de Joseph*. He will be far better in it than Nijinsky could ever have been.'

This absolutely enraged me. It was most wrong for him to speak like that, but he naturally felt very bitter about Nijinsky's marriage and tried to diminish him now. It was Nijinsky for whom this ballet had originally been written by Hoffmansthal and the music commissioned from Richard Strauss. Nijinsky had spoken to me about it and had described how the banquet was going to be all stylised – not one naturalistic movement would be allowed. Alas, that he did not do it, it might have been a masterpiece. Fokine's version was one of his dullest ballets, only redeemed by the beauty of Massine and his remarkable portrayal of Joseph. The Parisians wickedly called this ballet *Les Jambes de Joseph*, alluding to young Massine's rather big thighs. It was an altogether unsuccessful season. Fokine lacked inspiration, and his *Midas* was only acceptable because of Doboujinsky's beautiful décor, and his *Papillons* was a watered-down *Carnaval*. But *Coq d'Or* was glorious and lit up the dull season.

Vera persuaded me one day to go to a lecture by Professor Henri Bergson. I never liked lectures, but this time I hung on his lips – I had never heard before, nor have since, anybody speak of such abstruse things with such clarity and enthusiasm – he lifted you right out of yourself and made you hear the music of the spheres. His lectures became too celebrated and society ladies used to send their footmen to occupy a seat for them during the preceding lecture (poor mutts) – so that real students were often crowded out. The day I was there one of these ladies rushed at Bergson after the lecture, seized his hand and, holding it to her heart, cried, 'Maître, you were wonderful!'

He tried to free himself and muttered: 'Not at all, Madame, not at all.'

'Yes, yes, you were. It is *I* who am telling you.'

At this time I often used to go to a salon held in a house in the Boulevard Lannes by a lady whom I shall call E.S. She had a reputation for abducting young men at her parties, so much so that one virtuous young man could hardly be persuaded to come to her house at all.

'You must come,' said one of his friends. 'Her parties are always very amusing.'

'No, I don't want to be exposed to her advances. I don't relish the idea at all.'

'Don't be silly. You can always say no to her and get out of it.'

So in the end he was persuaded to go. In due course Madame E.S. began to talk to him, and eventually she was seen to lead him away, presumably to her bedchamber.

When he eventually reappeared, looking somewhat crestfallen, his friend asked eagerly, 'Joseph?'

'No,' he replied, humiliated, 'Jonah.'

I was still pursuing my career as recitalist and worked very hard on new programmes. For my holiday I went to Geneva where Dalcroze staged the Festival Vaudois for the bicentenary of the Canton de Vaud, using the lake in several tableaux. I stayed with Dr Leon Weber-Bauler and his family. He was an old friend, who had been married to Maria Yakunchikova, the brilliant Russian painter, a member of the group who worked with Diaghilev, Bakst and Benois on the magazine *Mir Iskustva*. She had died in 1902, but the house was still full of her works. Dr Weber-Bauler had travelled much, he had married in Russia before settling in Switzerland, and he wrote a wonderful book in most exquisite French describing his adventures: *De Russie en Occident*.

We had very gay parties in the evening, but towards the end of the month we could not help a feeling of anxiety creep-

ing over us all with the imminence of war. I decided to hasten
to Paris to be with my aunt, for I knew her husband would be
immediately mobilised. I managed to get a seat on the last
train and arrived in Paris on 1 August. No one would change
my Swiss money into francs – there was an awful distrust
about foreign money and terror about life generally. On my
way to my aunt's from the station I suddenly found myself
stuck in the traffic facing a fiacre in which Vera Donnet was
sitting surrounded by hat-boxes and starched blouses, fetched
at the last minute from the laundry, for she was always very
elegant. From the middle of all her luggage she called out
urgently to me, 'You must come to London at once, *at once.*'
Then the traffic began to move and we parted, she hurrying
to catch a train, and I hurrying to see my aunt and uncle
again.

I found that my uncle had already been mobilised. He was
to serve at the Front in France during the whole war, except
for some six months in Serbia where he volunteered to go to
fight another enemy – typhus. My aunt sent her two children
to Brittany but refused to go there herself. Her friends
brought her a ticket and implored her to come with them.
But she argued that with all the doctors at the front there was
the utmost need for women doctors to remain in Paris.

After a few days one got used, as one always does, to the
war conditions, and I resumed my lessons with Madame Rat.
But of course there was no possibility of recitals. The news
from the front became worse, and presently the Germans
were approaching Paris. The government advised everybody
who could leave the city to do so.

My aunt wanted me to go and join Vera, who was in
London and was calling me in every letter, and I myself, in
my cowardice, was but too glad to get away. So standing in
the train I arrived in Calais to board the boat. There was a
crush of thousands of people who wanted to get on, and,
being small and mobile (and ruthless) I managed to push

through. A wonderful sight greeted me there: on the deck, sitting on a trunk as if on a throne, was the great Chaliapine, beaming with happiness, having got all his children and young wife safely round him. And so I came to London in September 1914 and have lived here ever since.

I HAD been earning my living in Paris, but everything was finished there now, and I had to find a new livelihood. I went once more to see the Inghams, and asked if they could find me work. They were always very kind and solicitous, and I think they looked up to me because I was a dancer and therefore interested in every type of movement. Mr Ingham was a teacher at the Merchant Taylors' School (what extraordinary names English schools have!) who had taken Dalcroze's theories to England and was now director of the London School of Eurhythmics.

He immediately found me work in the school teaching the technique of movement – a subject which so far had never before been taught there. In addition to that I was sent out to various private houses where I taught small groups of children. One of these classes contained the names of almost all the members of the Cabinet at that time: there were two granddaughters of Prime Minister Asquith, Helena and Perdita Asquith; two sons of Reginald McKenna (Chancellor of the Exchequer), Michael and David; Winston Churchill's daughter, Diana; the Liberal leader Walter Rea's son Findlay, and Peter Scott, the son of the Antarctic, as we called him. The classes took place in their various houses in turn, so I often found myself in Whitehall. At one lesson all the parents who had lunched with the McKennas came into the drawing-room to watch their offspring, and I have a clear memory of seeing Churchill's very round, red-haired head.

But in 1915 with the Zeppelin raids most of these children

were taken away to the country. Only Peter Scott remained
in London with his mother and joined another of my classes.
He was then a little boy of six, and even at that age he was
already interested in birds. He once gave me as a present a
little tiny book which he had made with pictures of birds and
his own comments underneath them. There was a picture of
a cock under which he had written, 'The cock is a very noisy
bird.' And on the next page was a hen captioned, 'But the hen
is more so' – which I find astonishing for so small a boy.

Lady Scott had a cottage called Shingle End, very near the
Kent coast at Sandwich, where I sometimes stayed. Once
when she had gone back to London I remained there with
Peter and Winkie, his governess. In the evening I looked out
of the window and saw a Zeppelin flying in over the coast.
Peter was very excited and wanted to stay watching out of
the window long after his bedtime.

There was an Army camp with anti-aircraft guns near the
cottage, practically all around it. One day I was walking by
the camp with Winkie and Peter and talking to one of the
officers – who belonged to the Black Watch – when we heard
a noise far up in the sky and I asked him what it was.

'That's a Taube,' said the officer, and I looked up at it,
because I had never seen one before. Then suddenly a soldier
came rushing out of one of the huts, dashed up to the officer
and said something to him so quietly that I couldn't hear what
it was. The officer immediately shouted, 'Scatter, take cover!'

In a second the soldiers had gone. Everybody had to go to
his post or to a shelter. There was no question of them looking after three civilians. We were left quite alone.

Winkie and I couldn't at first make up our minds where to
go with Peter, and there was now nobody to ask advice from.
In the end we decided it was probably best to take shelter in
the cottage. Meanwhile the anti-aircraft guns had begun to
fire, making the most frightful noise, and when we got in-
doors the dresser was jumping about and the crockery was

falling down and getting smashed. There was no real shelter, but a little door led to two or three steps going down from the dining-room. So Winkie and I sat on the lowest, feeling that we were nearer to the ground there than anywhere else, and squeezed Peter between us to protect him in case something happened. We weren't hurt, but afterwards we learnt that quite close to us a bomb had struck the field-kitchen and had killed the cook.

Fairly early in the war – I think it was in 1915 or 1916 – Jaques Dalcroze came on a brief visit to London. On the outbreak of war the Germans closed his institute at Hellerau. He himself was a Swiss, and therefore a neutral, but his school was absolutely international and many French people were there.

Some of Dalcroze's pupils began to teach his method in Paris. Among them the most brilliant was Paulet Thévenaz. He was a very beautiful young man who was much beloved by Cocteau. He had illustrated a little book for children with the national anthems of all the Allies and correspondingly amusing designs. I remember learning the Japanese national anthem from it. But, alas, years later, in one of those fits of tearing things up that I have from time to time, I stupidly destroyed it and threw it away.

That summer Dalcroze came over with Paulet Thévenaz and a party from his school, and we all met together, with the English pupils, one Sunday at the Inghams'. It was a wonderfully gay evening. Dalcroze played on the piano, improvising with genius, and making a quite new kind of sound – real music – by laying newspapers, and even spoons and forks, on the strings of the piano to alter the tone. He could make music out of anything. He improvised songs, making up the words as well as the music, and we all sang them.

He even made a speech in English. He didn't know a word of the language, of course, but on some occasion in England, perhaps on this visit, he had agreed to respond in English to a toast at a dinner. And at our party he showed us how he did it. When he spoke, it sounded so like English that you were convinced that he was speaking the language but that you had somehow just failed to catch what he was saying. (It is a gift that Frederick Ashton has. He greeted me once in the street in such perfect Russian, with such a perfect accent, that I would have sworn that it really was Russian, but that I had not quite caught the meaning. Yet I knew he could not speak ten words of the language.)

On the Monday after that memorable party we all went to Kew. There was nobody there, the great lawns and avenues were empty. Someone of our group took a photograph of us. Now I can only recognise on it Dalcroze, Thévenaz and myself. The sight of those big empty avenues excited my usual impulse to do cartwheels. I find them intoxicating, they clear the brain and make you feel alive – I should like to do cartwheels every day of my life. So I launched out on a race with Paulet. We went cartwheeling down the avenue side by side. I remember the laughter and the clapping as people cheered us on, but I'm not sure who won. Probably it was Paulet, because he was at least a foot taller than I.

In London I went to have lessons with Serafima Astafieva. I had known her in Diaghilev's company, where she used to entertain us with her flashing and bawdy wit. She was a very good teacher and produced that wonderful first pair of English ballet stars, Markova and Dolin. At that time there was no question of making a dancing career with an English name, so Alice Marks and Patrick Kay adopted Russian ones and subsequently formed a brilliant partnership.

In addition to classes I continued to work on a new programme. Vera Donnet had an idea for a ballet for me which would be more than a series of separate dances. The theme was to be the awakening of the medieval world to the Renaissance. She wrote an excellent scenario for a ballet in two scenes, to be called *Pomme d'Or*. The first scene was in

Fra Angelico's style, with the figures seen against a golden background. Fiammetta prays in a chapel but her attention wanders from the words of the prayer to Beato, the beautiful monk who sings it. Their eyes meet and he drops the cross. Besides Fiammetta and Beato there were children choristers.

The second scene, with a Botticellian background, represented the earthly paradise Beato saw in Fiammetta's eyes. She tempts him with an apple, a golden one with which the children, now in wisps of diaphanous silk, had played at the beginning of the scene. He succumbs and they dance a sort of bacchanale.

Vera, who had great knowledge and sense of style, saw it all clearly in her imagination. But she could not do the choreography. So I had to arrange the dances in the right style. Everything I tried was too reminiscent of Eurythmics, the sort of thing that Cocteau wittily called 'Le Spectre de Dalcroze'. I was in despair.

Just then it happened that my great friend Mrs James Muirhead in whose house I lived all through the war, suggested that I should come with her to meet Mabel Dolmetsch, the wife of the famous Arnold Dolmetsch, who was a great expert on old instruments and the archaeology of music. Mrs Dolmetsch had never had any formal training in dancing, but she had studied the early sources from *Orchesographie* by Thoinot Arbeau (1588) to Feuillet (published in 1701), and with the help of contemporary glossaries reconstituted the Follia, Forlana, Volta, Galliard and other dances of the sixteenth century so beautifully that, in spite of her technical shortcomings in movement, the dances had a most authentic character. I once took Massine to see her, and he was very impressed and moved by her reproductions of old dances.

I immediately began to study with Mabel Dolmetsch, and when I showed the dances to Vera, she too was enthusiastic and said that it was the very style we needed for *La Pomme d'Or*. We went to various museums to study the pictures of the period, and at last we began to make progress.

The original theme of La Follia had been used by Corelli for his twenty-five variations, and they proved ideal for the first scene of our ballet. For the second scene, of which the characters had to be very different, we had music specially composed by a young man called Yelin. The set and costumes were by Vera Donnet.

There were only two dancing parts. I danced Fiammetta, of course, and Beato was danced by Jean Varda. He was a young Greek painter and not really a trained dancer at all. I had met him in Paris at the very beginning of the war when we were both queueing to register for our identity cards as aliens. Then he came over to London and had an exhibition of collages. But in 1917 he was almost starving, so I taught him to dance enough for a mimed role. Beato's part was made to measure for him and was carefully designed to include only the movements he could carry out, so he danced it with credit.

I had spoken about *Pomme d'Or* to Beryl de Zoete, who had been at Dalcroze's school after I had left and had since become a friend of mine. When she saw a rehearsal she was quite carried away and said it must be shown at the Stage Society (the original one), and took me to meet its Chairman, William Lee-Matthews. He too was very interested and decided to present it in the next programme – they only did four programmes in the year – along with John Masefield's *Good Friday*.

Our first performance was at the Garrick Theatre on 25 February 1917. The success was enormous and the critics were enthusiastic. A photograph of me on two whole pages of the weekly *Sketch*, as well as in other illustrated papers, made me appear – with Vera Donnet's superb make-up and costume – infinitely more interesting and better-looking than

I really was.* So when people gave parties for me and I walked in as my real self the guests could not hide a look of disappointment. I told them that I heartily sympathised with them, and we made friends.

C. B. Cochran, the famous impresario of the time, engaged us to appear in a quadruple bill on 16 March at the Ambassadors Theatre. Among the three plays was Anatole France's *The Man Who Married a Dumb Wife*, translated by Ashley Dukes, who was to become my husband – so our two names appeared in the same notices before we ever met.

And we did meet that same year on 7 August at a dinner at Mrs Lee-Matthews's. In the course of dinner, she turned to Ashley and said: 'By the way, did you ever manage to get the money out of that agent of yours?'

'No,' he replied, 'the wretch still owes me more than a hundred pounds.'

'What did you say his name was?' I said, for I wasn't sure I had caught the agent's name, and in any case we were speaking French, which I still found easier than English.

Ashley told me.

'Oh,' I said, 'but he's my agent too; and he owes me twelve guineas.'

I had danced at the Grafton Galleries for Lady Muriel Paget, who had arranged a Russian Exhibition for charity. Jean Varda, Hilda Bewicke and I had done some Russian dances there, and we were due to be paid something by way of expenses.

So Mrs Lee-Matthews said: 'Then you should go and tackle him together.'

* Soon after we were married, I had a letter from Ashley in which he wrote, 'We were called to a midnight conference in a ruined château. In the basement I saw your big photograph from the weekly *Sketch* pinned to an easel. I asked the fellow to give it to me, but he said, "I rather like the girl, so why should I give her to you?" I didn't admit that she was my wife, but after some bargaining I obtained the photograph at the price of six Kirchner girls.'

'Certainly,' said Ashley, who was in uniform and on leave from the Western Front, and he added with a conquering air: 'I will go armed with my sword.' In fact it worked miracles, and we got our cheques.

In this way fate brought us together as a direct result of our professional lives, Ashley because of his plays and I because of my dancing.

We met again next day for lunch, and for tea, and for supper at the Café Royal, where I met his friends, Epstein, Nash and other artists, and we spent the following day at Hampton Court. Then his leave came to an end, and he had to go back to France.

Many many years later, after Ashley was dead, I happened to find among his papers some sort of military identity card. It was dated 8 August 1917, the day after we first met, and I was staggered to see that he had put me down as his next-of-kin. I could not believe my eyes. Ashley had never mentioned it to me, never once boasted of his extraordinary vision in knowing, after only one day, that I would always be his next-of-kin. I looked at it, and checked it to make quite sure I wasn't dreaming. Then I put it away somewhere particularly safe, and I am still searching for it.

Before I met Ashley, who was then a captain, I had known no end of second lieutenants, for I was listed by many hostesses as 'the vivacious Mademoiselle Rambert', chiefly on account of my volubility. They took me out to luncheons and dinners in the most expensive restaurants, eager to spend the first money they had earned – (Oh Lord, how they had earned it!). As I am a small eater I could not help them that way, but I'm afraid I cost them a lot in keeping taxis waiting and they felt very grand paying with pound notes. I chiefly enjoyed going with them to revues, which were very good, and I didn't have to talk all the time.

How different was Ashley! He was a mature man of thirty-two, cultivated, knowing all about the theatre, having admired

Diaghilev's and Reinhardt's productions. He could speak many languages and was witty in all of them. But he was a poet too, as he proved in his writing.

He studied chemistry and physics at Manchester University. But after graduation he completely lost interest in these subjects and went to Germany to read philosophy in Munich. Having completed his education he was a tutor for a while, travelling on the continent, and then became a dramatic critic. His first play, *Civil War*, was produced by the Stage Society in 1910. As early as 1911 he wrote a book, *The Modern Dramatists*, which was years ahead of its time. Only the other day I lent it to the director of Nottingham Theatre who was amazed to find that it was written so long ago, so up-to-date it was.

He loved books, not only the reading, but also the sheer delight of handling them. He told me how, before the war, he once went into a quiet country church where the Bible lay open on the lectern. So, just as if it had been a book on a friend's shelf, he went up to it and began to read. He became absorbed, turned over the large leaves, and, as he would do in a private library, felt in his pocket for his pipe. It was only when he was about to light it, the moment when every smoker must look at the match, that he realised that while he had been reading the congregation had begun to drop in and were looking at him in amazement.

During that late summer of 1917 we corresponded almost every day for three months. At that time we spoke French together, and his first letter to me began: 'Ma belle marquise, j'éprouve maintenant ce besoin d'écrire qu'on appelle *cacoethes scribendi* dans presque la seule langue que vous ne parlez pas – ou est-ce que je me trompe?'* We met for another two days (he had to spend part of his leave in Bridgwater with his parents) and then we corresponded again for another

---

* 'My beautiful marquise. I feel now that need to write which is called *cacoethes scribendi* in almost the only language that you do not know – or am I mistaken?'

four months. Then he wrote to me: 'These two-day leaves are no good. But if we get married I will get four weeks. What about it?' I replied: 'Hurrah!' and we were duly married on 7 March 1918.

At the marriage ceremony, after we had signed our names, I asked the registrar whether, in view of my being a Russian subject with a Russian passport, there were any formalities for becoming British. He said:

'Madam, you *are* British!'

Without a second's thought I exclaimed: 'God save the King!'

My husband was very proud that this new-born British subject's first words should have been so appropriate, though I should hasten to add that when we first registered at an hotel, he said: 'Mind you put your nationality as "English" and not "British". I don't want to be taken for some damned Irishman or Scot.'

We were married in the morning, and the wedding break-fast was given by my darling friends the Muirheads. In the evening we were invited by other friends to their marvellous house, Aubrey Lodge. They gave us a magnificent dinner, at which Ashley and I each sat on a kind of raised throne – mine was decked with orange-blossom.

I refused to go away on our honeymoon, I'm ashamed to say, because my tailor-made going-away suit wasn't ready. We were married on a Thursday, and it wasn't going to be ready till the Monday. So we had to wait!

We agreed that we should stay in London at the Berners Hotel, because Ashley felt that all the smart officers would be at the Savoy, and a family hotel, near his own flat in Mortimer Street, would be much nicer.

But at the end of our gay evening at Aubrey Lodge we couldn't go to the Berners Hotel by taxi because all the taxis were on strike. So we went by tube from Notting Hill Gate to Oxford Circus. When we arrived there, we found that people were pouring into the station. The air-raid warning had gone, and Zeppelins were expected within three or four minutes.

Ashley looked at the hordes of people and said, 'Do you want to stay here with all this dreadful crowd, or will you run with me to the Berners Hotel? It won't take more than two minutes.'

'I'll run with you *anywhere*,' I replied.

So we ran until we reached the Berners Hotel. There we found all the guests sitting in the lounge on the ground floor sheltering from the air-raid. The officers were in their pyjamas and their wives in their boudoir caps. So we had to sit there with them for half an hour or so and foolishly hope that no bomb could penetrate the upper floors of the hotel.

That night there were several hundred casualties. It was one of the worst raids of the war.

When we did get away on our honeymoon we went to Bath. I had never before travelled first-class. In our compartment there were two officers sitting behind their *Morning Post*. One lifted his head, dropped his monocle and drawled: 'I say, is Bulgaria in Rumania?'

The other one dropped *his* monocle and drawled in reply: 'Ah, there you have me.'

Ashley chose Bath as he wanted me to see the most beautiful town in England. I was indeed enchanted with its wonderful style, the elegance of its buildings, the grace of its crescents, and I was quite staggered when we visited the Roman Baths. I had never seen anything like it before. We spent a fortnight there and then went on to Torquay to fatten up with Devonshire cream. I wonder how they got it for me as the war was still on.

Everywhere on that holiday there were those propaganda posters showing a small child lifting its head to its father and asking, 'Daddy, what did you do in the Great War?'

Ashley said: 'If ever a brat dared to ask me that I would give him such a spanking!'

Six years later, when my daughter was three, I made her ask him just that. He drew himself up smartly and said: 'I was with the machine-guns.'

Our married life, which started after four days of personal meetings and seven months of correspondence, lasted forty-one years – not unclouded happiness, of course, but always a wonderful companionship.

In the last years of his life we had four grandchildren who became the greatest link between us, and we all mourned him deeply when he died in 1959, just before his seventy-fourth birthday. But this is anticipating our whole life together.

I can never do justice to the way Ashley supported and helped me and encouraged me with his vision of what we could do together. I only realise now, and realise it every day, how deeply he understood me, my temperament, and how he foresaw my difficulties to come and tried to prepare me to fight them.

33. Ashley at forty

34. Our wedding photograph

35. As Fiammetta in *Pomme d'Or*

FROM MADONNA
TO MARQUISE

36. In *Fêtes Galantes*

WHEN our four weeks were over, Ashley had to go back
to France, the war went on, and I continued teaching with
occasional appearances at music-halls. I was even due to dance
an acrobatic *pas de deux* in *Lilac Time*. Meanwhile I had also
been appearing in some more ballets.

After the first happy achievement of *La Pomme d'Or*, Vera
and I were fired to do some more ballets with the same little
group. She had the idea of a ballet in Watteau's style to some
Mozart music to be called *Fêtes Galantes*. It had sober costumes, not in the usual powder-puff style, and with no little
buds and bunches of flowers. The girls wore silver-grey
taffeta of impeccable style, and my dress had one single rose
to the corsage. The wigs were beautifully carried out in the
most perfect eighteenth-century style, and the boys wore
mulberry-coloured ribbed silk. Seeing the sketches I quickly
tumbled into the right style for the dances and the make-up.
This had to be very special and an absolute contrast to my
make-up as Fiammetta in *Pomme d'Or*. There, for a quattro-
cento face, I had to blot out my eyebrows completely and put
on some very thin ones quite a bit higher, also the mouth was
made to look thinner. On the other hand in *Fêtes Galantes* an
absolute contrast was required: thick eyebrows and a very
full mouth copied from Madame de Pompadour.

On Ashley's second short leave I had to go to Soho for a
fitting of my powdered wig and I arranged with him that he
would call for me outside (the inside was too sordid, though
it was a master wig-maker's) in half an hour's time. Actually

I could not get away for nearly two hours and was distraught at the thought that he might rightly have lost patience. But he only said, 'It does not matter how long I wait, so long as you come in the end.'

After *Fêtes Galantes*, Vera and I worked on a ballet with Hilda Bewicke. Vera found her an exceptionally interesting dancer and suggested her dancing with me and Varda in a ballet commissioned by Lydia Kyasht. Hilda Bewicke was a most remarkable woman, whom I had known when we were with Diaghilev's company. She came from a very Scottish family, but she seemed completely cosmopolitan, because of her extraordinary gift for languages. She is one of the very few people I have ever met who can speak more languages than I can – and much better, too. She seemed to be able to pick up a language from the air. Polish and Russian without an accent were as fluent as English. She spoke Arabic and Persian, and I'm not sure that she didn't learn Sanscrit. Because of this gift, and her impeccable tact, she was always the one whom Diaghilev chose to sit in the Royal box when foreign Royalty attended, so that she could entertain them in their own language.

Once Hilda was in the Royal box with King Alfonso of Spain and his mother Queen Maria Christina, and they were all served with drinks. Hilda had a cognac au marasquin with a cherry in the bottom. When she had drunk it she inadvertently failed to stop the cherry from falling into her mouth. And it had a stone in it. So there she sat with the stone in her mouth. The others knew that it was there, and she didn't know what to do with it.

'I missed the psychological moment,' she told me, 'when I could have passed it off lightly with a joke and said "Now what does one do when one has a cherry stone in one's mouth?" And there it remained until the performance was over, and everybody was aware of it.'

She was a distinguished dancer as well as a remarkable

woman, and Diaghilev was devoted to her. Nevertheless she left his company twice during the war to go and be a nurse. She went with Lady Muriel Paget's contingent of nurses to work in dreadful conditions on the Russian front. Once they were stuck in a train with a load of wounded for three days without water. They had to dry the bandages in the sun because there was no water to wash them.

When she returned to Diaghilev the second time, he said: 'She is the only woman who has ever cuckolded me.'

Lydia Kyasht, who had been several times a guest artist with Diaghilev and was a delightful ballerina, settled later in London where she was adored. A great peer, who was very much in love with her, named his favourite racehorse Queen of the Ballet (by Royal Realm out of Lady Lightfoot).

During the war she invited Hilda Bewicke and me with my partner, Varda, to dance with her in Bournemouth at a concert which her agent had arranged. For this she wanted a new ballet, and Vera and I decided to do one to Chopin's valses and call it *Les Élégantes*. Once, when we were dancing in Bournemouth with Dan Godfrey conducting, Kyasht had a tiff with him at the dress rehearsal over some trivial business point. She became incensed and decided that we should walk out – she knew full well that the house was sold out and he would have to recall us. And he did, of course. He apologised to Kyasht and said:

'You are a very charming woman, Madam, but you are not a business woman.'

Thereupon she, quick as lightning, with her lovely Russian accent: 'Ah, but it is my *beesiness* to be charming.'

About this time Vera was also responsible for my first success as an actress. The Stage Society was putting on *The Provok'd Wife*, a Restoration comedy by Vanbrugh. William Lee-Matthews told me that the French maid was just the part for me, and asked me to play it. Vera's help was invaluable to me, as I had never acted before. She was a very gifted and experienced producer. She produced plays with Edith Evans and Nicholas Hannen in her time. And now she produced me. I studied the part with Vera giving me all the cues. She taught me every inflection and went over it again and again. And she made me a beautiful costume. I had a delightful scene with Lady Fanciful – acted by Ethel Irving – in which I was trying to induce her to go to a rendezvous:

> *Lady Fanciful:* Curiosity's a wicked devil.
> *Mademoiselle (turning to the audience):* C'est une charmante sainte.
> *Lady Fanciful:* It ruined our first parents.
> *Mademoiselle:* Elle a bien diverti leurs enfants.
> *Lady Fanciful:* L'honneur est contre.
> *Mademoiselle:* Le plaisir est pour.

There was another scene when I had to flirt with the valet, Rasor. I found this very difficult at first because there were some horrible rude words that I did not wish to say on the stage. They weren't so very dirty really, but I had been taught they were dirty when I was a child, and so they remained rude for ever. I know some swearwords in Spanish, and when I say them to Fred Ashton for a joke he shudders, because he was taught that they were dirty words when he was a boy. But in return he teases me with some dreadful words in Polish and Russian which he learnt when he was with Ida Rubinstein.

My part as Mademoiselle was a great success. Some of the critics thought that I really was French. And I had wonderful notices, though it was only a fairly small part, and the leads were taken by people like Mary Clare, Ethel Irving and Baliol Holloway. But I had neither desire nor ambition to be an actress. I needed movement above all.

When Diaghilev brought his company to London in the autumn of 1918 he asked me to dinner at the Savoy, where he always stayed. He told me all about Nijinsky's mental illness with genuinely great sorrow. He described the symptoms with lurid details and told me that Nijinsky sometimes crawled on all fours – which sounded more tragic than anything one could imagine: that flying spirit reduced by implacable illness to cling thus to the ground.

Later Diaghilev remarked with a half-smile: 'You know how Lady Ripon adored Vaslav and regarded him almost as a son. She was already preparing to have you as daughter-in-law.' I think Diaghilev pretended that he would have liked it to have been so. He never forgave Romola for having taken Nijinsky away from him.

During that visit we saw the brilliant works and wonderful dancing of the young Massine, who had now taken over all Nijinsky's parts and created many new ones. Without being a great classical dancer he yet had a wonderful stage presence as well as poetry and humour. This was the period of his character ballets, such as *Le Soleil de Nuit*, with Larionov's lovely setting and costumes, *Contes Russes* to Liadov's music, *Les Femmes de Bonne Humeur* after Goldoni, with music by Scarlatti and incomparable decor and costumes by Bakst, and many others. *Boutique Fantasque* came at the end of that same London season.

At that time Massine's dancing partner was Lopokova, a delicious little person of irresistible charm. Her humour gave a special edge to her poetry and vice versa. Seeing her dancing with Massine in *Boutique* has remained unforgettable.

She married that famous economist, Maynard Keynes, and was adored by 'Society' as well as 'Bloomsbury'. Once, soon after the war, I had tea with her at Gordon Square, and then we went in a taxi to the Coliseum where she was dancing with Idzikowsky. Half way there she stopped the taxi and ordered it to return to Gordon Square. She explained to me that she had to fetch a letter of her husband's, as she never moved without something – however small – of his. I asked her whether she had read his *Economic Consequences of the*

Peace, which had just appeared, and whether she understood it. She replied with ecstasy: 'Mim, there is no need to understand it, for me it is just like Bach.'

People adored her broken English, and, though she had quite a good vocabulary, she sometimes deliberately broke it for their benefit. Once, on a hot summer weekend in the country, she heard all the guests complaining of being bitten by harvesters. She half-remembered the word, and when next day the hostess asked her if she had slept well, she said: 'Not very. My bed was full of barristers.'

Another time, as she was going in to a luncheon party, and the butler had opened the door, she called out loudly to the hostess who had just appeared: 'Florrie, do you know that bats menstruate?' Even I did not know *that*!

Maestro Cecchetti had also come over to London with the Diaghilev Company in 1918. English pupils flocked to his classes. He taught non-stop from nine in the morning to six in the evening. Usually at about twelve somebody would give him a cup of chocolate and a banana, which he dispatched in a second, ready to resume his whistling. We never had any other accompaniment to classes. It was more convenient than a piano accompaniment, since the Maestro had no need to stop the pianist if he wanted to make a remark, or touch – quite hard – the guilty party with his stick.

When two years later I opened my own school, I followed his example, whistling away merrily – or crossly – but without the stick, as I always did all the exercises myself with my pupils.

All the pupils in Cecchetti's classes, who were not actual members of Diaghilev's company at the time, had to give him a guinea on Monday for the six lessons of the week. These guineas went straight into his pocket. As classes were very large and there were six of them a day, he made a lot of money. He got very offended when in due course a request for income tax reached him. He thought it was called 'École tax', and when anyone mentioned it, he shouted abuse: 'I am not a cheesemonger to keep accounts!' Then a second request came; and we tried to persuade him to fill in the forms, but without success. The third letter contained something about 'contempt of court'. Those of us who understood the gravity of the situation tried to persuade him to comply.

'Sit down,' he ordered me in French, 'and write these words: "Dear Sirs, Far from feeling contempt for your laws, I admire them very much. Here" – by now he was in a fury – "is a five-pound note, and not a sou more will you get from me . . ."' Finally we had to get a solicitor to deal with this impossible situation.

His use of language was fantastic. In one phrase he would mix three languages. He would scream, 'De andere kep!' *De* was his form of the English *the*: *andere* was *other* in German; and *kep* was *capo* in Italian. The gist of it was 'Turn your head to the other side!' There was one girl at whom he always shouted 'Colonna di Pisa!' But she, poor girl, had never heard of Pisa, let alone the tower, and so could not know, that he was trying to tell her that she was leaning slightly to the side, when trying to balance.

Lest these stories should seem to diminish the stature of Cecchetti, I wish to state quite categorically that he was the greatest ballet-master of his time. All the great dancers of the period had been his pupils, he himself having been a pupil of the great Lepri (heir to the historic Carlo Blasis). Pavlova allowed herself the luxury of private lessons with him when she was still at the Maryinsky. Later she had him as ballet-master for her company for several years and always worked with him. And, of course, the whole of Diaghilev's company profited from his daily lessons.

Cecchetti's classes naturally attracted émigrés who had fled from the Russian Revolution. Here they found friends who could talk Russian and might listen with sympathy to their tales of woe. Princess Meshchersky told us how, when she was fleeing from Russia, she hid her jewels by sewing them into the hem of her skirt. And then she had to wade across a stream: 'And all our clothes got wet and the diamonds and pearls beat against our legs – And you have no idea how painful it was!'

Towards the end of his period in London Cecchetti got it into his head to hold examinations of the English pupils at his school. I believe the real aim of this unexpected decision was to get Pavlova to come and see his pupils, and he persuaded her to act as one of the judges. I was to be another, and there were two more. I sat next to her. I hardly looked at the dancers (whom I knew anyhow and didn't particularly admire) for I couldn't take my eyes off her marvellous foot.

Pavlova shared Isadora Duncan's genius for communicating her ecstasy directly to the audience, although the means they used were absolutely contrasting. Isadora's movements were simplicity itself. Yet she could reveal herself completely through them. Pavlova had the great technique needed to dance ballets of three and even five acts at the Maryinsky. People in the West only saw her in excerpts from those ballets, then in single 'numbers' and even these became fewer and fewer in the course of her non-stop tours. Her technique gradually deteriorated under the strain of dancing eight times a week. At the Maryinsky a prima ballerina danced no more than two or three performances a month; the rest of the time was devoted to study. At that time she rivalled Kchessinska the Assoluta.

She had resigned from the Maryinsky after having tasted the delight of escaping to freedom in a few small tours with some other artists of her choice. She decided to form her own Company and to direct it herself. Any direction from above became irksome to her. Even with Diaghilev she could not bear to do one complete season. He wanted her to create the Firebird, for which Stravinsky had written that incomparable score. But she needed absolute liberty to give herself completely to the audience by her own means. No matter how poor the music and the décor, it was only her own dancing that mattered. That was what the whole world came to see. Her spirit came straight across the footlights and lit the world for us. We were not lookers-on – our souls were dancing with her, as they had danced with Isadora. André Levinson said of her: 'In the curve of Pavlova's instep are expressed all the yearnings of the Russian soul.'

I stayed on with my dear friends the Muirheads all through the war. Their daughter, Mrs Mabel Hopkins, has been a close friend all my life. They lost both their sons in the war, one on the Somme in 1916, and the other in 1918. The recollection of those ghastly telegrams that had torn their hearts and mine, became an even worse nightmare for me after my marriage. I could not believe that Ashley would come out of it all alive, and always dreaded finding that fatal brown envelope on my desk.

But at last the Armistice came. Ashley, who had always been a heavy smoker, announced to his mess that he was going to celebrate the occasion by giving up smoking. On the first day he was utterly miserable, longing for a smoke all the time. On the second day he had a dreadful headache. On the third day he bitterly regretted his decision, but was ashamed to give in so soon – so he held out. After that it became easier, and within a week he did not mind any more.

When he came home on leave in December, I was quite alarmed when I first saw him. It seemed as though something had been shot off his face. The cigarette was missing!

Soon he became a real fiend against smoking – even more of an anti-smoker than I. I remember once we met a strikingly beautiful woman at a party.

I said: 'Could she be as marvellously intelligent as she is beautiful?'

But Ashley said: 'The woman is a fool.'

'Why? How can you say that?'

'Can't you see she is smoking?'

And that was argument enough for him. He had become an anti-smoking fiend!

Ashley was not demobilised at once, for he had to serve with the Army of Occupation on the Rhine. At last the glorious day came, and I began to look for a flat to welcome him in our home. After five months of vain searching we at last found a flat on the first floor of a house in Kensington. Ashley had no job to come home to, as his pre-war job as dramatic critic on the *Evening Standard* could not wait five years for him. Fortunately James Muirhead and his brother decided to publish an English guidebook – the original German Baedeker was taboo – and they asked Ashley to write the chapters on the Western Front. This was the first of what became the famous Blue Guides. So he went every day to their office to write it while I went off to give my classes.

During my long married life I have not only never cooked a meal, but never even ordered one. From the very beginning Ashley said: 'I can see that housekeeping is not your forte. So let's invest our first income in a good housekeeper.' We had several inefficient ones, until in 1932 Helen Whelton came to us and has been here ever since, making my life easier and happier and becoming my great friend.

Cecchetti continued giving classes. And I went on going to them even though I was pregnant. When I reached the fifth month, it was just too much for him to have me there. I was trying to do *fouettés*, but he said, 'Stop it! Go home! I don't want a child born in my class-room.' So I had to give up going to his lessons, but I went on practising at home and giving my own classes.

One Wednesday morning I gave a class as usual. In the afternoon I had to give a private lesson somewhere in Hampstead. I went there by myself, and when I had finished the private lesson and was about to go home I suddenly felt

terribly lonely. It was something quite extraordinary, a most
dreadful feeling as though of cosmic loneliness. I felt quite
alone in the whole wide world. I have never experienced anything like it before or ever after. So I rang up Ashley to fetch
me – which I never would have done otherwise. Ashley drove
me that night to the hospital, and the next day the child was
born. We called her Angela because she was expected on
Armistice Day and we wanted a name suggesting peace.

At that time we only had the flat on the first floor of
Campden Hill Gardens, with a kitchen on the top floor where
the landlady lived. She objected to my child having her lunch
upstairs with the cook in the kitchen, and sent Ashley a note
forbidding it. He wrote back: 'This is part of my flat, and my
daughter shall cry in whichever part of the premises she
chooses.'

The birth of my second child, Helena (Lulu), was much
easier, I continued to do cartwheels right through pregnancy.
One week the doctor found that the child was the wrong way
up, and began to be concerned about it. But she had righted
herself next week, so clearly one or other of us had done an
extra cartwheel.

Soon after Angela was born we took over the flat above,
and when Lulu came we took the ground floor as well. So then
we had the whole of the house, and continued to occupy it for
forty years. I live there still.

I N 1920 I collected the various private pupils I had into a class and began teaching professionally. Like all teachers, at first I taught what I had learnt from my master. When you start to teach, you can quite easily correct those faults which your own teacher originally corrected in you, remembering how he had explained them. But when you come up against unfamiliar faults in your pupils, you have to discover by yourself the special exercises each pupil needs to get rid of his individual weaknesses, so gradually I found my own way of forming dancers.

I taught by insisting on the classical line with all my might. This line is almost geometrical in its precision and to such a degree a standard of perfection that the slightest deviation is immediately visible as a fault. When I saw a pupil continually repeat the same fault I tried to understand why he did so. Why did it happen? Sometimes it happened because they were too lazy to do well. Sometimes it happened because they were too anxious to do well, and sometimes because they were too ambitious, sometimes because they were too contented. In this way I tried to read their characters. And if they had originality and strength of character I knew that the more I insisted on their doing a classical exercise the more their inner being rebelled against that line and sought to find a line of their own. My absolute insistence on the classical correctness gradually produced a conscious rebellion which gave each choreographer his own style. My own exercises were very academic, and I stuck to them deliberately. I had no ambitions to create choreography. But I am quite sure that this discipline helped to develop the personalities of such creative artists as Ashton and Tudor.

When I was auditioning a dancer I looked of course at the build, the proportions, the hands and the feet and the eyes. It is in the eyes that the soul is reflected. They are the criterion by which one can judge an artistic temperament. That was how I chose my pupils – and I have seldom been wrong – most of them became artists in some sphere related to dance.

I have a reputation of having been very severe, as a teacher, and cruelly revealing their weaknesses. But this was not intended, it just sprang out of my heart and brain in my passionate endeavour to obtain the result needed. I was not aware that my words were often wounding. But they bore fruit, and nowadays when I meet my old pupils they quote those cruel, but most apposite, words, and we laugh together.

Although I love teaching the sheer technique of movement and taught it passionately, I also loved from the very beginning the work of production – the effort to obtain from the pupil his own way of saying in movement what he felt, and make it eloquent, like words. So I taught them various dances from Diaghilev's repertoire, and they sometimes performed them for guests at the studio.

Usually my classes were mixed, for I did not have enough pupils or enough time to divide the boys from the girls, and in any case the main part of the class is exactly the same for both.

Once a friend who was very much a *dame du monde* came to watch one of these mixed classes for the first time, and I said: 'Isn't it wonderful how the same classical exercises make a woman's body more womanly, and a man's more manly?'

'Yes,' she said, pointing to the fifteen-year-old youths, 'and the boys more boily.'

Once I was asked to arrange a dance for three beautiful women for some important charity in a big theatre. The

women were Lady Diana Manners (now Cooper), a famous
beauty both then and now, Rhoda Birley and Leslie Jowitt.
They none of them had had any dancing lessons. The object
was to show off their beauty and the magnificent dresses,
made originally for a costume ball, and copied from Velas-
quez's Infanta. For my dance the music was Ravel's *Pavane
pour une Infante Defunte*, and as it was rather long I used part
of it as an *ouverture*. When the curtains rose, Diana was revealed standing alone in the pose of the Infanta. At the dress
rehearsal, which was crowded, a unanimous gasp went up:
'How lovely!' Thereupon Diana, in a loud stage whisper:
'Who said "How lousy?"'

In 1921 Diaghilev decided to present Petipa's masterpiece
The Sleeping Beauty. He had by then lost Massine, who had
married, and had no new choreographer. He loved Tchaikovsky, and the idea of a full evening's ballet pleased him. Moreover, his English friends thought he might have a long
continuous run with that one ballet. They took him to see *Chu-
Chin-Chow*, then in its third or fourth year. Though the spec-
tacle appalled him, he was impressed by the fact that the
English public could stand such a long run. If his *Sleeping
Beauty* could last even for one year, it would give him a
chance to discover and form in the meantime a new choreographer. A long continuous run was unknown in Russia,
where all the theatres played repertory. On the advice of his
English friends he altered the title to *Sleeping Princess* so as
not to confuse it with the famous Christmas pantomime. He
invited Nicholas Sergueeff to teach the Maryinsky version and
Bronislava Nijinska to produce it. The gorgeous costumes
and scenery were by Bakst at his best, and the cast included
the finest Russian dancers available. But the public did not
respond. In fact there was no great public for ballet yet.
Diaghilev's own public was very small – enough to fill the
theatre for some seven to eight weeks in the year, no more.

And even this public was not ready to accept a full-length classical ballet. They found the story childish, and the steps seemed to them monotonous and meaningless, for at that time they had no idea whatever of the classical technique – nothing like today, when any member of the ballet public will hold forth airily on this dancer's 'arabesque' or that dancer's 'double-tours'.

Even today few people realise that the purely classical ballet is a totally abstract art. The story of it is told in mime and *mise-en-scène*. The actual dances are combinations of lovely movements and poses which convey no emotion in themselves, only delight in their beauty. And is not that enough?

In Russia a prima ballerina was allowed to insert her favourite variation (solo) into any ballet she chose. Diaghilev himself took advantage of this liberty in the production of his *Sleeping Princess*. He gave the role of the Lilac Fairy to Lopokova and Nijinska in turn. Instead of the variation which Petipa wrote for the Lilac Fairy, he took from *Casse-Noisette* the ravishing dance of the Sugar-Plum Fairy. As for the legitimate Lilac Fairy variation, he gave it to the tall and majestic Tchernicheva.

Not only the ballet *The Sleeping Princess*, but even the music of Tchaikovsky was considered old-fashioned at that time, in spite of the enthusiastic praise of the composer which Stravinsky wrote for the programme.

And so this glorious *Sleeping Princess* proved a complete fiasco, and Diaghilev went penniless from London, leaving the incomparable Bakst scenery and costumes behind to pay the debts of the season. Just twenty-five years later the English public was ready to acclaim this ballet, and it is in the repertoire constantly.

It seems incredible today that such a great work of art, so perfectly produced, should have got so little recognition. The dancing alone, quite apart from the superb production, was of the highest quality, with Spesivtseva as the Aurora of incomparable beauty and technique, and the rest of the cast worthy of her. Diaghilev admired her even more than Pavlova. At the dress rehearsal, finding that the powdered wig was unbecoming to her, he ordered it to be removed – a grave offence to Bakst who was a past master of style and had the whole cast in wigs. But Diaghilev maintained that her beauty was all important and won.

There were four other ballerinas to share the role with her: Trefilova, Egorova, Lopokova and Nemchinova. I admired them all, but Spesivtseva's performances were the ones I never missed.

Spesivtseva was a dancer of infinite grace. She came once to my school as I was giving a class, and I happened to ask her something about Le Spectre de la Rose. There and then, just as she was in her town suit, she showed us how it should be danced, in such a way that you felt all Fokine's choreography coming alive. And then, just as naturally, she showed us the peasant pas de deux from Giselle.

At the Maryinsky the uniform for a ballerina was quite unvarying. She had to wear pink tights and pink satin shoes and a tutu. The tutu might have slight variations; for instance if you danced a Greek dance it might have a Greek key-pattern, and if you were in an Egyptian ballet you might have scarabs on your crown. But until, under the influence of Isadora Duncan, Fokine rebelled, there was always a tutu, and the tights and shoes were always pink.

A notable exception was made by Spesivtseva, who decided that in the second act of Giselle, when she rises from the grave, she would be dressed all in white, including white tights and white satin shoes. It was more otherworldly and more touching. Spesivtseva gave me once one of her white Giselle shoes (a ballerina never gives a pair of shoes when asked for a souvenir and I treasured it). Alas, I lent it to some exhibition, and I never got it back.

Egorova, one of the five Auroras, once had some trouble with her knee and asked me if I knew a good masseur. Ballet dancers usually have their favourite masseur whom they recommend to one another, and everybody goes to him until someone recommends a better one. So I recommended one Henry Boyd, a cockney who had very clever hands, and arranged an appointment with him.

I went there with Egorova, and when we arrived at his house (he didn't have a separate clinic), and knocked at the door he came out and looked at us in surprise, because I hadn't told him there would be two of us.

'Weren't you expecting us?' I said.

'I were.'

So we went in. It was an extraordinarily dirty place, with retorts and phials on the shelves as if it was Doctor Faustus's laboratory.

He took Egorova's leg and began to massage it, and as he rubbed her knee he said: 'There hought to be a hoil hoozin' hout of Madame's knee, but that hoil is missin', and that's why Madame is in pyne.'

Vera Bowen and I had always been seen everywhere together. Then suddenly we broke off and did not speak to each other for several years. The cause was a misunderstanding so trivial that we could hardly believe it could have estranged us for so long. During that period, although we both were present at almost all Diaghilev's performances, we stood in the intervals in separate groups. A common friend of ours summed it up, commenting on this situation: 'There stood Vera at one end of the foyer surrounded by her court, and at the other end Mim surrounded by her soviet.'

Ashley had by now long finished with the Blue Guides and was working in the theatre again. He had been responsible for Kaiser's *From Morn till Midnight* being produced by the Stage Society, despite the objections of some of the actors to a play by a German author. And in 1922 he went to Germany to see the playwright Ernst Toller in prison. Angela and I joined him on the Baltic coast, and we all went on a shopping spree in

Berlin. It was the time of frightful inflation in Germany, and it seemed as if for our twopence you could buy something worth ten pounds. We felt awful about it, as if we were robbers. But we succumbed to the temptation and spent our money. Ashley bought a pram and a high-chair for Angela and goodness knows what else. We had practically no money left. We just had our tickets home. At the frontier they wanted us to pay so much duty on the things we bought that Ashley had to hand the pram over to the customs officer. Then on the train Ashley left his hat in the restaurant car. As soon as he remembered he went back for it only to find that the restaurant car had been uncoupled and left in some siding. So there he was without a hat, and at that time without a hat nobody would trust you. If you belonged to what was called the 'Hatless Brigade' you were supposed to be quite disreputable. Nobody would cash our cheques, and all the officials were rude. At Brussels we had just enough to pay our bill, but we could not afford a tip. We had to steal away leaving the exact money with the bill on the reception desk. Our boat tickets were of course already booked and paid for. And so at last we arrived in Dover penniless and very hungry. Ashley said, 'You and Angela had better wait for me on the beach. I'll go and try to find rooms. When they see we have luggage they'll probably trust us and give us supper, and then I'll get money from London.'

So the baby and I stayed on the beach. We were both terribly hungry, and we looked enviously at people nearby having a picnic. Everybody always brings too much food for a picnic. Soon they were throwing sandwiches at one another, and even cakes.

Angela looked at them and said, 'Mummy, I want a cake.'

'Go and ask the lady,' I said.

So Angela toddled over to them and came back with her hands full of cake. And I ate half of it, I am ashamed to say. At last Ashley returned, and everything was all right.

A couple of summers later, when we were holidaying in Normandy, we went to Calais to meet an English friend. While Ashley went to the Customs with her, I suddenly saw Dalcroze about to get on to another train.

'Où est ton Achille ?' Dalcroze asked as the train was starting.

I very much wanted him to meet Ashley, but Ashley had not yet returned from the Customs. Disappointed, I went outside the station to wait in the car. Suddenly Dalcroze's train came back – it had only been a false start. And at the same moment Ashley appeared on the platform. So I stood up in the car and whistled a tune by which I knew Dalcroze would recognise me, and as he turned to look at me I shouted 'Voici mon mari!'

He shook hands with Ashley and said: 'Monsieur, as a dramatic author you should not have married a wife who whistles!' (in French *siffler* also means to boo) and jumped into the moving train.

At Easter in 1925 I went with Ashley to Monte Carlo. I wanted to have some more classes with Maestro Cecchetti. I was going to ask Diaghilev to give us guest tickets, but Ashley stopped me. His principle always was: 'If a play is worth seeing, then it is worth paying for. Otherwise how would stage artists live ?' But when Diaghilev saw us standing at the box office he called us away: 'Nonsense, don't be silly – you are my guests for as long as you like.' So we went all through that fortnight.

Picasso was there too. One night, when he and some friends were waiting with us for Diaghilev before the performance, he looked into the distance and said musingly: 'No sign of Diaghilev's *ménage* yet . . .'

But he came, of course, and, of course, with Kochno.

I heard Picasso speak only once more, and that was when he mocked my wonderful authentic Chinese cloak (a gift from a very rich pupil, but most unsuitable over my fashionable evening dress): 'Vous voilà en Empereur de Chine.'

One evening when we had supper with Diaghilev he asked Ashley. 'Who is this young writer who has had such a success with his play?'

Ashley said: 'Do you mean Noël Coward?'

'Yes, yes, I do,' said Diaghilev.

'I should say an English Sacha Guitry perhaps?' (It was still at the beginning of Coward's brilliant career.) And the conversation continued with Diaghilev very interested in the English theatre. What a pity he did not know that Ashley himself was about to make an enormous dramatic success at the Haymarket!

During that fortnight in Monte Carlo Diaghilev happened to see me once in a restaurant lunching with Anton Dolin. He flew into a jealous rage – though by that time he was already firmly attached to Lifar – and he did not answer our greeting. From that day till the end of our stay he never addressed a word to me. Nevertheless, I was not going to leave Monte Carlo without thanking him. But he cut short my thanks by saying ironically: 'Et c'est toujours le premier danseur classique, n'est-ce pas?' He was still sore about Nijinsky.

In 1925 Ashley had a great and unexpected success. When he and I had corresponded almost daily in the late summer of 1917 he told me of a plan for a play he had thought about for a long time, and he sent me a synopsis. Indeed he originally intended it for Nora Charrington, Janet Achurch's actress daughter, an intimate friend of his who had died in 1914. The plan for the play was deceptively simple. There were four travellers – a lady with her maid and a nobleman with his man. They meet at an inn, and you expect that the nobleman will pair off with the lady and the man with the maid. But the play develops very differently. It is the nobleman who takes the maid. And the lady responds to the passion of the man.

The Man with a Load of Mischief as Ashley eventually called it was poetical and subtle in its themes.

He wrote about his play afterwards: 'Producers for instance

were talking of Shakespeare in modern dress; but this was to be modern thought in a period setting . . . its speech, though without any gadzooks, was to fit the dress and the setting.' The language is indeed well-chosen and witty as well as profound. There is a proverbial wisdom in such phrases as 'Many friendships have been lost by being claimed' or 'Men reason to strengthen their own prejudices and not to disturb their adversaries' convictions'. And I have always liked 'Our fortunes, like our clothes, have been made to measure and fit us tolerably well.' However, the simplicity and tenderness of the play, indeed its genuine poetry, counted for a lot more in its artistic success than its wit. The irony of a man already in love with a woman being commanded to make a pretence of wooing her is, as Ashley remarked, 'one of the classic though rare motives of comedy.' And there was something very touching in the lady stooping to the man-servant's 'hard sincerity in love'.

Ashley wrote the play in 1924, and it was at once accepted by a publisher. But at first nobody would produce it in the theatre. Later that year it was put on by the Stage Society with Fay Compton and Leon Quartermaine. It had an enthusiastic reception and brilliant notices. And in 1925 it was acquired by Frederick Harrison for the Haymarket, where it opened in June and packed the theatre for eight months – a long run for a poetic comedy in those days.

It was also produced in America, but there, instead of perfect Fay Compton in the role of the Lady, they gave it to a film star. Ashley cabled me from New York: 'THEATRE FULL – PERFORMANCE EMPTY'.

The royalties from *The Man With a Load of Mischief* seemed to us colossal. We had started married life together on Ashley's army bonus of £300, and we always worked hard – and with joy – to earn our living. We lived modestly, not coveting possessions. It was the unexpected money from the play – it amounted to £333 in one memorable week – that first gave Ashley the idea of some day building a theatre of our own. This was our common passion and all our spare money went towards achieving it.

Soon after Ashley came back from America the Bernard Shaws asked us to lunch at Ayot St Lawrence. Ashley had known the Shaws for a long time, but for me the prospect of meeting the great man was very exciting. I was to join Ashley at Paddington, but stayed too long at rehearsal and missed the train. Determined to get there, I caught a later train and still managed to arrive in time for lunch. When I entered the dining-room, I was staggered to see on the table an enormous roast chicken, looking almost alive. Mrs Shaw explained that she did not share her husband's vegetarian convictions. To please him, when I was offered the choice, I said I liked vegetarian food, and ate a ghastly, sticky macaroni, praising its delights.

Though the conversation was most entertaining, I only remember one story Shaw told. A friend of his was once before a judge on some censorship charge. In pleading for him his Counsel said he was a disciple of Tolstoy. The judge said: 'And who may that be?' 'A famous vegetarian, m'lud,' replied Counsel.

Some years later I met Shaw when I was going to Haslemere to hear a Dolmetsch concert and he was on the same train. He walked the half mile or so with me to the hall. He talked continuously the whole way, though I didn't follow a word. All the time he had his mocking Mephistophelean look, so I thought he must be saying something wickedly funny and looked up to him – I was half his size – with an amused smile. Suddenly he stopped, put his hand on my shoulder and said, 'And then she died.' I could have done so too.

I had a pupil, Frances James, who loved to arrange little ballets for various charity performances. I took no interest in them, but allowed her to use the other pupils. Once she told me she was preparing a new ballet about a water-lily. But that sounded too ordinary a title. She wanted to know the French for it, and I said 'Nénuphar'. The sound of that beautiful word suddenly kindled my interest, and I talked over the idea with her and advised about the costumes for the ballet which became *Nénuphar*. She used to design the costumes herself, and they were pretty but banal. This time I asked my friend Sophie Fedorovitch to do them. I had met her in 1921 in Cecchetti's studio, where she used to come and draw the dancers during classes and rehearsals of *The Sleeping Princess*. We became great friends at once. Sophie was an extraordinary woman, of high intelligence, talent and immense integrity, and with all that a genius for friendship. She was a Russian Pole and we always talked Russian, only breaking into Polish for a joke. She was a very small woman with a deep voice. She wore her hair very short, strikingly so, which made her look like a boy.

I showed Sophie our *Monumenta Scenica*, a series of big albums with reproductions of stage designs by Burnacini, Bertoli, and others from the Albertina Museum in Vienna. She felt very inspired by them and designed beautiful costumes – her first ones for the ballet.

About that time Ashley suggested to me the idea of doing a ballet on the story of Vatel, which he had just read that day in one of Madame de Sévigné's letters. Vatel was the renowned cook of the Duc de Montmorency. Once, when his master was expecting Louis XIV to dinner on the following day, Vatel prepared a special menu fit for a king. Unfortunately, the fish did not arrive in time from Dieppe and, rather than face the shame of one of his courses failing at the royal table, the passionate chef hanged himself.

The plot seemed to me good, but I thought it better in this ballet to make the hero a dress-designer rather than a cook. I felt, having seen Massine's witty play with spoons and forks in his ballet *Les Femmes de Bonne Humeur*, that we should keep clear of food. So we had Monsieur Duchic as a *grand couturier* who shows his newest collection to rich cus-

tomers, the Viscount and Viscountess Viscosa, the first manu-
facturers of artificial silk. They admire the *Rose d'Ispahan* in
pink satin, the *Désir du Cygne* in white, on blue, and other
creations, but are shocked by the one called *Le Sporran*, and
flee in disgust. Monsieur Duchic cannot survive the affront
and kills himself.

I thought that if I helped Frances James, we might together
evolve suitable choreography. For the role of Monsieur
Duchic I cast my only male pupil, Frederick Ashton. He has
himself described how he saw Pavlova in South America and
was fired with the ambition to become the greatest dancer in
the world. At first he studied under Massine, but could only
manage one lesson a week, as he had to earn his living in an
office. When Massine left for America he advised him to
come to me. We became real friends very soon, though he
was only eighteen. He had intelligence, wit and charm, and,
above all, one felt in him the born artist. He had beautifully
arched feet and an aristocratic profile. He ultimately justified
both. Though he had not the physical strength required
specially from a male dancer, he had the infinitely rarer power
to speak through other dancers and ultimately became the
greatest English choreographer of universal fame. But we
are still at the very beginning of his career.

Although he had no technique yet, he had unfailing grace
even when he was making mistakes in movement. He found
it very difficult to copy my *enchaînements* (sequences of dance
steps) to music, though he was genuinely musical. Later I
realised that as he was himself creative, the music probably
suggested to him subconsciously much more beautiful *enchaînements* than the purely educational ones which I combined.

I told Fred about the Vatel ballet and that I would like him
to dance Monsieur Duchic. The next day when we talked
about it, he did such wonderful movements, so right for the
character of Duchic, that I decided forthwith that he would
have to do the choreography. He was very reluctant, as he

had never before composed even a single dance. But I thought I had experience enough to help him.

The first thing to do was to find suitable music. Fred thought that we should commission a score from Poulenc or Auric. We had always had endless conversations about Diaghilev's ballets and went together to many performances. Nijinska's *Les Biches* and *Le Train Bleu* particularly impressed him. But I maintained that not only could we not afford these composers, but also that as a beginner he needed music which already existed, so as to have a score with a definite shape to follow, which would serve as pattern for his choreography. I searched for music for a long time, but Fred did not like any of it. At last I took some piano pieces of Eugene Goossens and arranged myself a dance to show to Fred. I never had the remotest talent for choreography, but I could *arrange* a dance to any music. I had to do many such arrangements for pupils going to auditions – but that was *not* choreography as I understood it.

Fred became interested in my tentative sketch and began to alter the movements so successfully that he turned it into an excellent dance. From then on he went straight ahead. I asked him how he meant to finish the ballet, for Vatel hanged himself, and that seemed too sinister an end for the light-hearted subject. Without hesitation he said: 'He will stab himself with his cutting-out scissors.' But I still did not want to end with just the corpse on the stage. Thereupon Fred found a brilliant solution. 'I will bring in the mannequins, and they will come and dance a lament for him.' I was enchanted with that idea.

Now came the question of décor and costumes. Again Fred wanted to do what Diaghilev had done for *Le Train Bleu* – have them designed by Chanel. And again I had to disappoint him, for two reasons: not only could we not afford Chanel, but even if we could I did not want a dressmaker – however brilliant for fashion clothes – to design stage costumes. I suggested Sophie Fedorovitch. She immediately produced beautiful designs of the right character and a perfect set representing a salon panelled with mirrors, with vague silhouettes of models reflected in them. Fred was delighted with Sophie's sketches, and she was very impressed by his talent for choreography. She was a woman of incorruptible integrity, spirit and tremendous understanding of art, and she helped him enormously. This was the beginning of their lasting friendship and subsequent collaboration in many ballets both for our company and the Royal Ballet.

One evening I met Nigel Playfair who asked me casually what I was working on. When he heard that we were doing a ballet to a synopsis by Ashley he became very interested, as Ashley's name was at that time on everybody's lips because of the enormous success of his *Man With a Load of Mischief* at the Haymarket. Playfair needed an extra item for his revue *Riverside Nights* which he was producing at the Lyric Theatre, Hammersmith. It had a brilliant cast and excellent sketches by A. P. Herbert and others.

We called our ballet *A Tragedy of Fashion*. I had the part of Monsieur Duchic's partner, Orchidée, and I was to wear *Le Sporran* which so shocked his customers. I smoked a cigar, and Nigel Playfair insisted that I should also turn cartwheels in this ballet. I was notorious for doing them on all ocasions. I had done them round Mozart's monument in Salzburg, in front of the National Gallery at midnight and in other improbable places. I had done three on the roof of the Princes Theatre during an interval at a Diaghilev evening. Nigel thought a kilt most suitable, and Sophie designed a ravishing Scotch ensemble. But I think it was ultimately altered for a more 'fashionable' one, since in all the photographs I am wearing a golden outfit with a mannish coat.

And so on 15 June 1926, I presented the first ballet by Frederick Ashton, *A Tragedy of Fashion*. It turned out to be the beginning of Fred's brilliant and fertile career, as well as the beginning of English ballet in the twentieth century. (Earlier there had been the masques of Ben Jonson and ballets by Weaver – but all this was lost and there was only music hall for showing ballet.) *A Tragedy of Fashion* ran for some months and as soon as it came off we felt the need to go on producing more ballets. Fred arranged several dances on Mozart's *Petits Riens* but we could not complete them then, as I was asked to produce the dances for Purcell's *Fairy Queen*, which was being done by Dennis Arundel for the Purcell Society, and of course I wanted Fred to arrange the choreography. In my memory still stand out three items: 'One charming night', the symphony while the swans come forwards, and 'Echo'. They all had very original movements perfectly in keeping with Purcell's glorious music.

In 1926 Ninette de Valois opened her Academy of Choreographic Art in London. I thought the name of the school too grandiloquent, but the prospectus impressed me very much. It showed great intelligence, immense knowledge of ballet and the theatre, as well as practical sense, and seemed to carry in it a promise of future great developments. It made me feel very small and ignorant and useless. I seriously thought that I should send all my pupils to Ninette and close my school. My depression grew every day until Ashley became quite impatient with my moaning and threatened to go to America for six months.

But just then I was asked by Ernest Thesiger to present my company at a charity show he was arranging at the newly opened Arts Theatre in Leicester Square. In my state of utter depression I wanted to refuse, but Ashley insisted that I accept.

Frederick Ashton had been offered an engagement in the newly-formed company of Ida Rubinstein in Paris for which Nijinska and Massine wrote ballets. He wanted this experience, and the money; he decided to go, and I was happy for him.

I arranged a programme out of the things we had in our repertoire. I was not dancing myself as I had usually done before, but sat in the audience watching my pupils dance on the stage, not just practising in the studio. I saw their performance with fresh eyes and couldn't believe what I saw, for they looked so different from other English dancers I had seen. They seemed to have real style and looked like real artists. I was so enchanted that I hardly realised that this performance was, so to say, the work of my own hands. When I did so, all my depression vanished and I forthwith developed a Napoleon complex and thought I could conquer the world!

Here were real English dancers. At the time when I first came to London the standard had been abysmal. I had visited several English schools and to my amazement saw little girls of three or four put into hard, real ballet shoes and running about on their points with contorted legs. But after the creation of The Association of Operatic Dancing in 1920 (later to become the Royal Academy of Dancing) the standard rose quickly and has gone on rising ever since.

Ashley had been commissioned by Matheson Lang to do a play from the then famous novel by Lion Feuchtwanger: *Jew Süss*. In one of the acts Süss gives a great ball at which the guests are entertained with a little opera. Ashley said to me: 'Neither you nor I know enough about opera, why not have a ballet instead?'

So I told Fred about it, and he immediately thought of a subject, *Leda and the Swan*, which could be all in white and thus stand out from the many-coloured costumes of the guests at the ball. Already at that time he had a marvellous sense of the theatre. He found that Gluck's music of the 'Blessed Spirits' from *Orpheus* would fit the subject well, and we began to rehearse. But Matheson Lang had to put off the production of the play till the following year. And in the meantime Fred went off to Ida Rubinstein.

In 1927 Ashley bought the freehold of a large church hall in Notting Hill Gate. He saw at once that if the hall were divided in two it could provide not only a studio of my own for my rapidly growing school, but also a small theatre for both of us. When the theatre came to be built, he had the excellent idea of adding a dimension to the very small stage, with its proscenium opening of no more than eighteen feet, by putting an apron stage around part of the front and building a staircase at the back. There was also a very small dressing-room where ten girls – even stars like Markova – all dressed in a line. I should never have thought out any of this without him.

To celebrate the opening of the studio (before the theatre was ready) we gave two large cocktail parties with over a hundred guests in each, and at both showed *Leda and the Swan*. Fred was still available to dance the swan, and a very beautiful pupil of mine, Diana Gould (now Mrs Yehudi Menuhin) was Leda. The choreography was charming and a great success. We also showed the completed *Petits Riens* with very inventive and Mozartian choreography by Fred.

That same evening, as always during his seasons, I went to see Diaghilev's company at His Majesty's Theatre. I arrived late, of course, after the beginning of the programme, and found Diaghilev in the foyer talking to Samuel Courtauld. Diaghilev stopped me and said: 'I hear that you have in your company a girl as beautiful as Spesivtseva. Why am I not invited to see her?' He was being friendly with me as

Courtauld had just told him about our company. He was un-
predictable with me (as with others), sometimes very warm,
at other times freezing.

I said that of course he could come whenever he liked to see
a class, but we were in the last week of the school term.

'Tomorrow I cannot,' he said. 'I see my doctor. Shall I
come Wednesday?'

'You cannot, you are lunching at the Belgian Embassy.'

(There was a puzzled look on his face. How did I know
about embassies?)

'Thursday then?' he suggested.

'I am afraid I have to give a lesson at a Teachers' Congress.'

'You and your Teachers' Congress! You just don't want
me to come – that's obvious.'

'Oh yes, I do, I will be delighted if you come on Friday.'

In my heart of hearts I almost wanted him not to come, I
was so afraid of his judgement – and my subsequent depression.

On Friday we were half-way through the class when he
appeared, accompanied by Kochno. I was with my back to the
entrance and suddenly saw Ashton go as white as a sheet.
(Later my little daughter reported: 'Mummy said that
Freddie went as white as a sheep!')

Diaghilev watched attentively, and at the end he said:
'That is all right, it is our good old Cecchetti. Now show me
something new.'

So Fred and Diana danced the Adagio from *Leda and the
Swan*. He was obviously impressed by Diana's beauty but
wondered if she might not grow too tall. I did not think so, as
she was already sixteen. (In the event he proved right.) He
said: 'When will she be ready?'

I thought another year at the studio was necessary, and he
agreed. I called her out, as he asked to talk to her.

'Will you come to us?' he asked.

'I am coming tonight with my mother,' replied Diana very timidly.

'No, I mean will you come and *dance* with us?'

She only breathed an ecstatic 'Oh!'

The next morning Fred and William Chappell, another of my dear pupils and a talented designer, left to join what they later called Compagnie des Répétitions de Madame Ida Rubinstein, as they rehearsed nearly eight months but gave very few performances in all. All those rehearsals with the great choreographers, Nijinska and Massine, were of the utmost value to Ashton in furthering his career.

In 1928 I was again in Monte Carlo. In the course of a luncheon with Diaghilev and Kochno – the hostess was Florrie St Just, a great admirer and friend of the company – Diaghilev said airily: 'And now we'll have to get Chirico to design a costume for Dolin that will cover him from head to foot – just as we had to uncover him for *Train Bleu!*' And he also said with a touch of mockery: 'And I will do *Swan Lake*, however much Vera may be against it.'

The luncheon was very rich, and Diaghilev ate a lot and also drank a lot, and when one of the two other guests made a remark to him about it being against his doctor's orders, he waved it aside.

To me Diaghilev's season of 1929 stands out as a peak almost as great as his very first season of 1909. There were nearly thirty ballets performed in the course of four weeks. We saw the best ballets of Fokine: *Les Sylphides*, *Prince Igor* and *Petrushka*; Nijinsky's *L'Après-midi d'un Faune*; Massine's *Boutique Fantasque*, *Tricorne* and his own version of *Sacre du Printemps* with Lydia Sokolova as the Chosen Virgin. She gave a powerful, unforgettable performance which would have made Nijinsky's heart leap with joy; then there were Bronislava Nijinska's frivolous *Les Biches* and her stark epic *Les Noces*.

And then there was Balanchine, by now a complete master.

Royal Opera House
COVENT GARDEN

Mr. Serge Diaghileff
requests the honour of the Company of

Mrs Ashley Dukes

to assist at the Final Rehearsal on

MONDAY, JULY 15th, at noon
at the
ROYAL OPERA HOUSE, COVENT GARDEN
of
IGOR STRAVINSKY'S Music
for the
"RENARD"
Previous to its first presentation in England
and the
CONCERTO for Piano
by
IGOR MARKEVITCH
Played by the Composer and the
COVENT GARDEN ORCHESTRA

12 Noon, Monday, July 15th   Cocktails 1 p.m.

37. Frederick Ashton. The inscription reads: 'To dearest Mim. In appreciation of whom I dedicate all the ballets done under her guidance. With love & homage. Fred. 1930.'

38. *A Tragedy of Fashion*, Sophie Fedorovitch's first set, with the great mirror flanked by gigantic scissors. In the centre, bowing to customers, Ashton and Rambert

39. M. Duchic and
Orchidée in *A
Tragedy of Fashion*

40. Sophie
Fedorovitch

41. Ashton and Pearl Argyle in the
opera box in *Les Masques*

42. Ashton and Markova in *Mephisto
Valse*

43. *Valentine's Eve:* in the centre Maude Lloyd, left Elisabeth
Schooling, Ann Gee, John Andrewes, Andrée Howard, John Byron,
Hugh Laing

44. *Leda and the Swan,*
1927. Ashton and Diana
Gould on the ground

45. *La Péri*, 1931. Costumes
by William Chappell.
Markova and Ashton in the
centre

46. *Foyer de Danse,*
Markova and Walter Gore
on the stairs

51. *Les Sylphides* at the Lyric, Hammersmith, 1930, with Karsavina in the centre

52. Karsavina reciting Pushkin to me

His *Apollon Musagète* (created in 1928 to music by Stravinsky) had a perfect décor by Bauchant, specially effective in the apotheosis, when Apollo leads the Muses up to Parnassus, and his chariot drawn by three steeds appears descending towards him. It was a scene of breathtaking beauty, unforgettable.

And then came Balanchine's creation for that season, his *Fils Prodigue*, with very new choreography on an archaic theme and a perfect sombre décor by Rouault. The passage when the Prodigal drags himself on his knees to beg forgiveness of his father, who opens his cloak to receive his son on his bare breast, was deeply moving, memorable. It had a simplicity, seriousness and almost solemnity of treatment which made me feel that Diaghilev, through Balanchine, was about to take a new road, and a warm human heart was revealed. It was the culmination of his achievement.

Diaghilev gave a midday party at Covent Garden for the dress rehearsal of *Renard*. The guests occupied two or three rows of stalls and we were greeted by Diaghilev who stood at the top of the stairs. We were treated to Igor Markevich, for whom he foresaw a great future, playing his new composition. He was adored by Diaghilev like a son. We then saw Lifar's *Renard* – his first choreography, which showed promise, but perhaps a little too much daring. And then we went up to the Crush Bar, and Diaghilev was, of course, a perfect host.

In the last days of the season there was a midday party in Dolin's studio (he was now reconciled with Diaghilev and danced in the last season). At some moment Diaghilev came up to me and asked me something – perhaps it was just 'And how is your life?' – in such a warm voice that I felt quite close to him, as never before, and we had almost a heart-to-heart talk. He looked so ill, with his leaden complexion, and so helpless. Where was the giant I had known before? I felt terribly concerned about him, and implored him not to be so reckless about his health. (I had heard by then about his diabetes, but he ate and drank everything that his doctor forbade.) He smiled pathetically – and that was the last I saw of that great man.

A few weeks later, when we were in Blackpool with Ashley's play *Jew Süss*, our cook came up to me with a newspaper and said: 'Isn't this the man you always talk about – Dgag . . . or something?' I looked and felt darkness close around me.

Now that Matheson Lang was at last ready to put on *Jew Süss*, we decided not to use *Leda and the Swan* in it, as we had in the meantime shown that ballet at a matinée at the Apollo Theatre (with Constant Lambert conducting), and also at another performance at the Savoy, arranged by Grace Lovat Fraser. So I turned to Ovid's *Metamorphoses* for a subject and found the story of *Mars and Venus*. It was most suitable for the act when the Duke returns from his victorious campaign and falls in love with the beautiful Naomi.

After long searching I chose three pieces of Scarlatti: the first was a dance for Venus with her nymphs arraying her, the second – the arrival of Mars, the third – the seduction and disarming of Mars.

Now that I had the synopsis and the music I went to Paris to talk it over with Fred, who was just finishing his engagement with Ida Rubinstein, and on his return he composed a short, but perfect, ballet: *Mars and Venus*. Venus was danced by Pearl Argyle. She was a creature of legendary beauty and a lovely sensitive dancer. Harold Turner, a brilliant dancer whom I had amongst my pupils soon after Fred's arrival, was a convincingly virile Mars.

The play opened on tour in Blackpool, of all places, and then came to the New Theatre in London. It was much praised, and so was the acting of Peggy Ashcroft as Naomi (her first big part), Felix Aylmer and, of course, Matheson Lang.

The company had a very good time in Blackpool. Ashley

and Peggy Ashcroft rode on the sands. (He missed the company of horses in peacetime. During the war, in the artillery, his horse Brutus was his great friend, he talked about him for years.) We all went to the funfair. On the Giant Dipper, I screamed with terror, but nobody took any notice or had any sympathy for me – they all thought I was laughing. Everybody else wanted to have a second go, but I said, 'No fear, not on your life.' And I wouldn't go. It was much the same at the swimming pool. Everybody was larking about and enjoying going down the water-chute. So I thought I ought to try it. I stood at the top, trembling with fear and cold. I absolutely froze. And people kept pushing past me and shooting down. And they all seemed to be so happy. At last I plucked up courage and down I went; and I couldn't get enough – it was so delicious. I must have gone down twenty times.

But our little ballet was not a success. It had only one notice – and that one was jeering. The critic called it 'A dance with skipping ropes. It had nothing to do with the play.' Originally Fred wanted rose garlands into which Venus would entwine Mars, but at rehearsals the garlands kept getting entangled because the dance, though beautifully composed, was rather complicated – so we decided to have thick silver ropes, instead. And this is what the critic called 'skipping ropes'. The notice ended with the remark: 'What a pity dramatic authors have wives, and those wives meddle in ballet!'

Undismayed, we continued to work at the studio, and Fred began to talk of giving a public performance of what was by now a professional company from our school. So I approached Nigel Playfair, who knew us well from *A Tragedy of Fashion*, and we fixed the matinée for 25 February 1930. Fred prepared a new work, *Capriol Suite*, to music by Peter Warlock – a series of sixteenth-century dances, but freely embroidered with beautiful choreographical inventions of his own, just as the original tunes had been treated by Warlock. It had excellent designs by William Chappell which were used for the following thirty years. Originally they had cost us only five pounds for the materials, which we sewed ourselves.

At the matinée we showed some variations from *Aurora's Wedding*, some dances from *The Fairy Queen*, as well as *Leda and the Swan, Mars and Venus* and *Capriol Suite*. It all was received very warmly, and Playfair offered me a fortnight's season at his theatre. He said we needed a star and advised us to approach Karsavina. I thought it would be too impertinent to ask her to dance with my pupils who were to her, the great ballerina, almost beginners. But he pointed out that she already had one of my pupils – Harold Turner – as partner in her series of recitals at the Arts Theatre. Incidentally, at about that time she published her book *Theatre Street* which was immediately recognised as a classic. A great dinner was given by the Critics' Circle in honour jointly of Karsavina, a ballerina who suddenly wrote a book, and Ashley, a writer, who put a ballet in a play.

So I went to see her in fear and trembling, but as always she was infinitely gracious and encouraging. The idea appealed to her, and we forthwith sketched out the programme. In addition to some items she had danced with Harold, and to her own lovely *Mademoiselle de Maupin*, she suggested doing *Les Sylphides* with Fred as Partner and a small *corps de ballet* of my dancers.

To have that great artist work with us was not only the greatest honour, it was also the greatest lesson, both in art and behaviour. Though the company was at that time only at the beginning of its career, she treated us all as equals. Once, during our first rehearsals of *Les Sylphides*, at the end of the Nocturne, when Fred stood in the centre with Karsavina on one side and Diana Gould on the other, holding them both by the wrist, they had to remain in an attitude balanced on point for a second before moving away. Diana held her pose too long, imagining it to be a test of balance. I shrieked at her in horror, but Karsavina said to her very gently, 'You look at me, Diana, and I will look at you, and we will come off the point together.' I could have cried at such graciousness, I who was so rough. Another example of her exquisite manners, so unlike the proverbial prima ballerina: she said to me, 'Peggy Cochran asked if she might watch *Spectre de la Rose* from the wings.' To which I replied, 'And did you give her permission?' – assuming that she had. She said, 'I told her I would ask you – *you* are the director.' Again I was deeply moved. I realised how unhumble I was – alas, incurably.

Ashley suggested that we should do a ballet on the theme of *Le Jongleur de Notre Dame*.

It is an old story – medieval or earlier. There is a miraculous statue of the Virgin, to which the devout bring offerings. Some acolytes come with their gifts. One brings a scroll of poetry, another brings a carving, a third comes with a musical instrument, and so on. The juggler watches it all – he loves the Virgin as much as they do, and longs to make his offering too. But there is only one thing he can do and that is a handstand. The monks are horrified and rush forward to stop him, but at that moment the Virgin drops her veil in sign of grace, and everybody is transported by this miracle and they all sing Ave Maria.

I asked Susan Salaman to tackle this subject in the setting of my old *Pomme d'Or*. Susan was a sister of my pupil Merula (later married to Alec Guinness) and had previously written for her a little children's ballet, *The Tale of a Lamb*. I was the statue of the Madonna, Harold Turner was the nimble juggler, and Fred Ashton the lute-player. The ballet was very good, and the touching story was told in movements of poetic simplicity. The music of Respighi could not have been better if it had been specially commissioned. At the first performance we even had a Russian choir for the moment when everybody burst out singing (they had been engaged by

Playfair for another programme, so we could not resist the chance to use them).

All this combined into an excellent performance and we had enthusiastic notices and sold-out houses. The mother of one of my pupils said in her enthusiasm, in the foyer, 'That Madame Rambert is like Diaghilev.' Whereupon one of my waggish friends whispered: 'Yes, Mim *is* like Diaghilev, she prefers the boys!'

Ashley, with his usual spirit of enterprise, began to talk of a season at Christmas. Diaghilev's London seasons were usually in the summer, but Ashley thought that London might like ballet during the festive season too. How right he proved!

Edwin Evans, the musical critic, was enchanted with *Capriol Suite* and invited Fred to do a ballet for the newly formed Camargo Society, thus named to avoid the more appropriate name of 'Ballet Society'. The word 'ballet' was not familiar yet, and many jokingly suggested that some people might call it 'Bally Society'! Who would believe it now?

At their first performance Fred did *Pomona*, which was his seventh work since *Tragedy of Fashion*. Thus he already had a good deal of experience in choreography, and *Pomona* was a small masterpiece.

In 1932 the Camargo Society gave a season at the Savoy Theatre, the dancers for which came from de Valois's and my companies. In the course of that season, sixteen ballets were performed, including three classics; the second act of *Swan Lake*, the complete *Giselle* (both these ballets with Spesivt-seva), and a two-act version of *Coppélia*. The rest of the repertoire included de Valois's beautiful *Job*, to the music of Vaughan Williams, book by Geoffrey Keynes and designs by Gwen Raverat after Blake.

For the Savoy season Ashton was asked to do the role of Job and I the part of Job's wife. Somehow we were utterly unable to learn the roles. We were both by now so used to

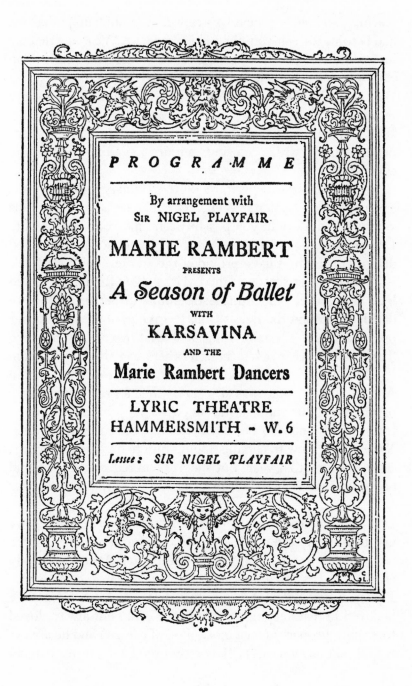

PROGRAMME

By arrangement with
Sir NIGEL PLAYFAIR

MARIE RAMBERT

PRESENTS

A Season of Ballet

WITH

KARSAVINA

AND THE

Marie Rambert Dancers

LYRIC THEATRE
HAMMERSMITH - W.6

Lessee: SIR NIGEL PLAYFAIR

teaching and seeing ourselves reflected in our pupils that we had become too self-conscious to learn a part. We found that we just could not do it. After a few rehearsals we plucked up courage and declined. But for quite a while we were called 'Mr and Mrs Job'. The part of Job was taken over by my pupil John MacNair.

It was a very beautiful ballet, and I watched the first six performances with growing admiration for de Valois's choreography.

In 1933 all the repertoire of the Camargo Society was given over to Sadler's Wells. On that occasion de Valois wrote to me: 'Could you possibly lend me your boys again? I wish to goodness Job had had three sons and seven daughters, I could have provided the whole family myself!'

After my first season at the Lyric, Ashley thought it would be a pity to let our enthusiastic public disperse, and so we decided to found the Ballet Club to give performances in our own Mercury Theatre. I insisted that we used the word 'ballet' in the title, even though others had shied away from it. Ashley was appointed Director, and we also invited Arnold Haskell, who was already by then a great connoisseur of ballet and our enthusiastic supporter, to join us. Before the theatre was quite finished Pavlova came to see Fred's *Capriol Suite* with a view to commissioning him to do a ballet for her. Alas, she died that year. But she had entered our theatre, and had given us her blessing, thus consecrating the Mercury for ever after.

When we first started our Ballet Club performances we had to use my studio as a box office and green room. A year later the house next to it became vacant and Ashley promptly acquired it (as usual on a mortgage) and transformed it into a proper box office and an extra dressing room. He never believed in just keeping money in the bank, but always loved to acquire property (on a mortgage, of course) and he always would add sardonically: 'I borrow good money from them and will be glad to repay some day with bad.' He loved to transform a hovel into a civilised dwelling and let it to friends for just the equivalent of the bank rate.

When the second house adjoining our studio became free Ashley bought it too, and rebuilt the inside to provide a bar and to house our collection of prints. So now we had a proper theatre – of minimal dimensions but fully equipped for performances of both ballet and drama and even small operas (Pergolesi, Arne and others). The amount of these various forms of theatrical art produced there is astonishing, when one considers that only in 1943 did we obtain our first grant from CEMA (later to become the Arts Council). Even I am staggered at the amount and quality of theatrical art born on that stage, and with infinitesimal finance. I consider this the greatest tribute to Ashley's vision.

The theatre had only a hundred and fifty seats, plus standing room for about twenty-five. The stage was only eighteen feet deep, including the apron, and the proscenium also measured only eighteen feet.

Looking back, one can hardly believe that such miracles were performed in that tiny space and that Fred Ashton, Antony Tudor, Andrée Howard, Walter Gore and so many others created ballets for it. The proximity of the audience made it very difficult to create any illusion, one had to make a strenuous effort of imagination to produce works that would transport the audience away from reality into a world of fantasy. Absolute sincerity was required from the artist and complete identification with the part, as the smallest pretence would be felt by the audience immediately. It was a hard school for the choreographers, but it taught them to use every gesture imaginatively, every step, and of course every dancer. Later when Ashton began to create for larger stages it was much easier for him to obtain new effects with that experience behind him.

As for the dancers themselves, it required special virtuosity to make no noise whatever, and do in height what they could not do in width. After that, when they came on to a bigger stage, it gave them tremendous élan. People often think it is difficult to dance on a big stage after a small one, but it is not so. In fact the reverse is true. When the Bolshoi company came to Covent Garden, they found it very difficult to dance there. In three jumps they had crossed the stage and had to fill up the musical phrase with a pose instead of the fourth jump. Their stage in Moscow is much bigger.

Nicholas Sergueeff, who had been ballet-master at the Maryinsky, was now working as ballet-master at Sadler's Wells. Every time I met him he told me that there was something very important he wanted to talk to me about. So I invited him and his wife to lunch, and he told me all about a ballet he wanted to put on. It was a terribly trite story about a Rajah or a Sultan and all his wives. He insisted on telling me every trivial detail.

So I said, 'In what way can I help you?'

'Well,' he replied, 'I thought you might like to put it on at your theatre.'

'Why not at Sadler's Wells?'

'Oh, that's much too small!'

Here, at least, was someone who thought the Mercury was as big as the Coliseum.

Not only was our stage small, but at that time several of our ballets were very short. *Capriol Suite* lasted only ten minutes and *The Lady of Shalott* twelve minutes. So in order not to have intervals between these short ballets, our two magnificent pianists played interludes. When we went on tour, the audience, who naturally had come to see ballet, not to hear music, talked so much during these interludes that the pianists said they wouldn't play: 'Nobody wants to listen to us.'

But I said, 'You play beautifully, and I'm sure people enjoy it. We *must* have interludes. But I promise you I'll be in the stalls, and shush them down.'

I managed to quieten all the talkers in the stalls by glaring at them and saying 'sh-sh-sh', but still the talking went on up in the circle. So I went upstairs and started shushing there. But there were two women who just would not take any notice of me, they went on talking with great animation.

'How can you?' I said.

Then they turned round, and I saw that they were the two pianists' wives—they had heard them play quite enough at home.

We used to put up notices in the dressing-rooms at my school, usually a week before the end of term, asking the pupils to clear away their clothes. In spite of this they would leave masses of skirts, tights, shoes etc. We made big parcels and sent them off to the Rhondda Valley where unemployment raged in the late twenties.

One of my artists once said to me: 'We must go on a big tour of the Rhondda Valley.'

'Don't be silly, Walter, you know they are starving there. Nobody will buy tickets, so what's the point?'

'So as to teach the Welsh miners what the jockstraps are for!'

We began to collect members for our Ballet Club soon after our first season at the Lyric in 1930 and opened it in 1931. We had a second season at the Lyric, Hammersmith that same year and showed Fokine's *Carnaval*, revived for us by Karsavina and Woizikowsky, who danced the roles of Columbine and Harlequin. Fred composed *Mercure* to Satie's music of that name, and to his great honour and the ineffable delight of the public he had Karsavina dancing in this ballet as Venus. In 1931 he produced *Façade* for the Camargo Society, that brilliantly witty ballet to the perfect music which William Walton had originally written for Edith Sitwell's poems. The décor and costumes matched it all beautifully. The Society could just afford the costumes but not the complete set by John Armstrong. So I offered to pay for that and obtained the sole right to include this ballet in our repertoire. It required a minimum of rehearsals as it had been created entirely on our company, of which Markova was a regular member for four years. The only guest in the original production was Lopokova. At the Mercury she was replaced in the Tango by Markova.

For the same season Susan Salaman produced a short sketch called *Le Rugby*, our first ballet on a truly English subject. It was a great success, and Susan followed it later with *Le Cricket* and *Le Boxing*.

Harold Turner was brilliant in *Le Rugby*. Coming on stage with the ball, he was instantly stopped by three delightful fans: Pearl Argyle, Andrée Howard and Prudence Hyman, each wearing a rugby jersey over a tutu of a different colour. They implored him to give them his autograph. He signed in a hurry as the whistle blew and he disappeared behind the fence, on which was written 'Players Only' – the one bit of scenery. The audience did not see the game, but the fans watched it over the fence and expressed their excitement in delicious runs on points. Presently the whistle blew, and the player reappeared, his clothes torn to shreds, and proceeded to describe the game in a very realistic dance. There was a moment when the audience roared out in delight. I never understood why, but knew by the music when it would occur. I believe the incident had something to do with the scrum.

The same thing happened to me in *Le Cricket*. I understood nothing of the game, but could always tell when the audience was bound to laugh. It came at the moment when the ball was wrongly hit and went upwards. All the players watched it disappearing into the blue, and the audience loved it.

The third sporting sketch, *Le Boxing*, was also a great success and was easier for me to understand. All three sketches were done in pure dancing, yet were completely expressive of the essence of each game.

During all these seasons at the Lyric we used to bring Karsavina to my house to rest between the matinée and the evening performances on Wednesdays and Saturdays. My two little daughters had the supreme joy of being allowed to take to her: one an egg and toast, the other strawberries and cream, while I carried in the tea. She could relax and fall asleep and was as fresh as a rose again.

For the summer holiday we went as usual to Dymchurch, at that time an unknown village in Kent, warmly recommended – though under the seal of secrecy – by Sybil Thorndike, who always came there with her numerous family, as well as her brother Russell with his.

We loved our little Russet Cottage. Sometimes I had some members of my company to stay there for a while. Ashton came a couple of weekends. His antics on the beach were hilarious and most original. He would dive with the children's tyre, part his hair under water, emerge with the tyre round his head, two fingers of his right hand pointing upwards, call out 'St Luke' and disappear under water. He never repeated the same joke, no matter how much we pressed him, but had ever more amusing variations on that theme.

The children were very fond of him and called him 'Fled' – long after they knew how to pronounce his name properly. He gave the girls Beatrix Potter's *Peter Rabbit* inscribed 'Love from Fled'. Who could have guessed at that time that he would ever make a ballet film of it, and be such an adorable Mrs Tiggy-Winkle?

That summer of 1931 I had a call from Bronson Albery, who wanted us to fill in a week at the New Theatre. I did not want to accept, as we had nothing new to offer, and it would be our first appearance in the West End. But he proposed very good terms, and I accepted for the sake of the company. It proved a mistake.

While we were there we had an offer for a week at the Palace Theatre in Manchester. Both there and at the New Theatre Karsavina danced with us in the three Fokine masterpieces she had produced for us, *Les Sylphides*, *Spectre de la*

Rose and *Carnaval*, and they were her last performances before she retired from the stage. But the Manchester public were puzzled by the programme changing every night. A whole evening of ballet, however varied, was a completely unknown experience in the provinces at that time.

We had opened the Ballet Club on 15 February 1931 with a programme containing Fred's new ballet *La Péri* to music by Paul Dukas. We had engaged Markova, a brilliant young English dancer, who at an early age became a member of Diaghilev's company, where she rose to important roles. The sudden death of Diaghilev in 1929 left her without any artistic outlet, and she did not wish to appear merely as an item in the commercial theatre. Fred was very anxious to have her as a permanent member of our company, and she was a great inspiration to him during the four years she was with us. The first ballet he wrote for Markova was *La Péri*, and he was Iskender, who seeks to steal the flower of immortality from her.

The same programme contained the last of Susan Salaman's sporting sketches, *Le Boxing*. In it the flight of steps at the back of the stage, which led to the dressing-room was used for the first time. Ashley thought of those steps chiefly in order to add a dimension to the small stage – and they were used in many ballets for various purposes. Thus in *Le Boxing* the two champions, the American and the English, emerged in their dressing-gowns on the landing on top of the steps and saluted the audience before coming down on to the stage, which represented the ring. In *The Lady of Shalott*, they led to the chamber where the lovers retired. In *Foyer de Danse* the dancers came down to their classroom where their Maestro was already waiting at the barre, impatiently twiddling the cane which he was to use later to emphasise his corrections. In *Les Masques* the door on top of the landing was open, and a blue light from the batten, reflected in a mirror at the back of the dressing-room, gave the impression of geat depth to the stage. We later managed to do *Spectre de la Rose* on that stage. For the last leap Harold Turner flung himself in the air and landed in the arms of three boys who were waiting to catch him on some stairs outside, as there was no room at all in the wings.

The audience soon began to appreciate the special qualities of our performances and grew apace. They liked what the critic Ernest Newman described as 'the atmosphere of Versailles' there, with the elegant bar in a room surrounded by a remarkable collection of prints of dancers of the nineteenth century* and where one could drink the best wines – Ashley could always find those at the sales he frequented to stock the cellars of the Garrick Club.

In the thirties we used to go to Cambridge, to Terence Gray's Festival Theatre. By 'we' I mean myself and Ashley, who seldom missed a first night anywhere. Terence was an adventurous producer and always worth seeing. He also offered good wines in the hope of inducing the University to patronise his theatre. It was a new sort of *snobisme*. One night after the performance we had supper with Terence and his partner Harold Ridge. Ashley and Terence never stopped discussing the various *crus*. Harold leant towards me and whispered in my ear: 'Do you too, believe in all this vinous uplift?'

Terence often quoted Reinhardt, who said that to deal with actors you must put on surgeon's overalls. After a few years Terence got tired of the theatre and went to France where he acquired a vineyard to produce his own 'crus'. He even sent us a few bottles, which Ashley smiled at. After a couple of years, on a visit to London Terence came to dine with us. I said to him: 'So now you are happy not to have to deal with English actors?' He answered bitterly: 'The French peasant

---

* On my eightieth birthday I presented the whole of the collection of prints to the Victoria and Albert Museum in gratitude for all that England had given me. It is also a memorial to my husband and is called The Marie Rambert–Ashley Dukes Collection.

is even worse.' Later he abandoned his vineyard, took to breeding horses and won the Irish Derby.

At one of the many parties we gave after a performance at the Mercury, a young man, a friend of Ashley's, said to me: 'You need men like me to show your youngsters how to lift a girl.' So I said: 'Come on, show us.' In a second he picked me up without any preparation, lifted me eight feet off the ground (he was well over six foot himself) and then dropped me. Fortunately I relaxed in time not to break my legs.

Thereupon I proceeded to explain to him how a ballet lift is done. It does not depend merely on the man's strength, nor on the lightness of the girl. She is as much a participant as the man. It is her initial bending of the knees and pressing the ground with the whole foot that gives the spring which he exploits, adding his own strength to obtain the greatest height. But when the moment comes to descend, all his strength is needed to bring her down carefully and lightly. She cannot make herself lighter, it is he who must fight gravity, so that it all will look absolutely effortless.

This 'double work' has been developed considerably by the Soviet dancers. At the time of Petipa or even Fokine, the lifts were much fewer and lower. The Soviet dancers made them more spectacular, adding lifts on one hand only, with the girl remaining up there in various beautiful positions.

We were all staggered when people like Lapaury and Struchkova first showed those lifts. They seemed to us acrobatic. But now they have become an integral part of the art of 'double work,' and all choreographers use them, sometimes with great imagination.

In 1929 a young man who wanted to study with me had come to my house for an interview. He had fine eyes and looked a poet. We had a long talk, and I became deeply interested in him. He told me he could not come to classes before four as he was working until three, starting at 5 a.m. at an accountant's office at Smithfield Market. I was impressed by the fact that he was prepared to study dancing immediately on top of a ten-hour working day and accepted him as a pupil. His chief interest appeared to be choreography. He was Antony Tudor, and he became one of the most original and profound of English choreographers.

When he was only in his third year, he asked me to let him do a ballet. I smiled at that premature ambition but was pleased when he showed me an excellent synopsis of the garden scene in *Twelfth Night* and the music he had chosen, by Frescobaldi, an Italian contemporary of Shakespeare and therefore most suitable for the subject. I asked him to compose a solo and a *pas de deux* – if he contemplated such items. After a week he showed me Malvolio's entrance, duly pompous, and a really comic *pas de deux* for Malvolio, in crossed garters and an amazed Olivia danced by beautiful Maude Lloyd. On the strength of those fine dances I let him go on with this ballet, which he called *Cross-Garter'd*. It was not a good ballet, but showed enough talent to justify its inclusion in our second season at the Ballet Club in October 1931. It was much praised by Massine.

For that programme Ashton created a charming short ballet on *The Lady of Shalott* to Sibelius piano pieces. There was a gauze in front representing the mirror in which the Lady is condemned by a curse to see the world reflected. Pearl Argyle was the Lady, and Maude Lloyd, on the other side of the gauze, her very plausible reflection. There was a dance of reapers, then the lovers' dance ('I am half sick of shadows,' said the Lady of Shalott). But when Lancelot appeared she could not bear it any more and broke the mirror and fled into the real world. Her last drowning dance was most moving. At the end when everybody surrounds her corpse it was easy to imagine Lancelot (Ashton) saying: 'She had a lovely face. God in His mercy grant her grace.'

Ashton's next ballet was *Foyer de Danse*, inspired by Degas. He danced the Maestro, lovable, severe and funny. I have a little film of that ballet and one can see what a talented dancer Fred was at that time. Markova was brilliant as the 'Etoile', and there was a very gay *corps de ballet*, typically Degas.

In 1933 Ashton wrote *Les Masques* to Poulenc's trio for oboe, bassoon and piano. Sophie Fedorovitch designed the whole ballet in black and white with two opera boxes at each side of the stage and a tall white column against the steps at the back. (The column and the opera boxes were made of corrugated iron and painted white, and I well remember going to an ironmonger's in Shepherd's Bush with Sophie to buy it.) The synopsis told of a 'personnage' who goes to a masked ball with his lady love. His wife is there too, masked of course, and he is irresistibly drawn to her. At the final unmasking the husband and wife are staggered to recognise each other, and fall in love again. Poulenc's trio was played by remarkable musicians: Helen Gaskell (oboe), Cecil James (bassoon) and our permanent pianist Charles Lynch – for whose special sake Thomas Beecham often came with Lady Cunard to a Sunday night performance. Poulenc saw this ballet and was enchanted with it. He presented me with a copy of *Soirées de Nazelles* with an enthusiastic inscription: 'A cette chère Madame Rambert avec mille félicitations et un million de remerciements.' The whole of this production cost £60 including Sophie's elegant costumes.

These restrictions in material means forced the designers to stir their own and the audience's imagination and proved a fruitful school for Fedorovitch and all the other designers. Even at Covent Garden in 1946 she used the minimum of material for Ashton's incomparable *Symphonic Variations* and thus strengthened its effects. Hugh Stevenson, who also started in our blessed poverty, later designed many excellent décors for Sadler's Wells, and so did William Chappell and Nadia Benois, who likewise fledged with us.

Our dancers, in general, proved very useful to Sadler's

Wells, and I lost them one by one. They were paid there and had an interesting repertoire, so I could not blame them. For a short while they still had permission to dance in our Sunday performances, but soon the growing amount of rehearsals in both companies made this sharing impossible. They helped a lot at the beginning of Sadler's Wells, as they had all been produced in our very varied repertoire, including several ballets by Ashton, Tudor, and, of course, the classics taught to us by Karsavina. Although I had only about twenty professional pupils at that time (the rest were all amateurs and children) we managed to provide the Wells with: first of all Ashton, for whom as a choreographer the move represented a natural development; Pearl Argyle, who was their first Odette in *Swan Lake*, as well as having ballets written for her by Ashton and de Valois: Walter Gore and Harold Turner, who were respectively the original Rake and the original Dancing Master in de Valois's masterpiece *Rake's Progress*. Leslie Edwards was one of us too, and became an important character dancer at the Wells. It was all very good for them and thank heaven, we managed to replace them, one by one.

On top of all that, Elisabeth Schooling taught them with my permission the choreography of *Façade*, which Ashton, like all choreographers, could not remember in detail. Also William Walton was very anxious to have it performed with an orchestra. This, of course, was a painful parting from the monopoly we had of that perennial jewel of English choreography.

Markova too must be counted among the other benefits the Wells received from us. She had not been trained in our studio, but at Astafieva's. She came to us from Diaghilev with invaluable experience. But working for four years as a regular member of the company in Ashton's and Tudor's ballets, specially written for her, and the classics with Karsavina's stamp on them, made her a marvellous intrument for both the new English and the classical repertoire at the Wells.

I must apologise for writing all this, but so few people know the very hard path we had to tread, and the heartbreaks – I sometimes wonder how we managed to survive and always produce new dancers and even choreographers.

ALTHOUGH I have referred several times to the Mercury, we only gave the theatre that name in 1933. Before then it was known as the Ballet Club. On the occasion of its opening under the new name, Ashley wrote in the programme: 'Mercury being the God of commerce, it is strange that so few play-houses are called after him. We have nothing against his mercenary attributes, but we prefer to think of his dexterity and charm, his musical inclination and his dalliance with the nymphs (whence Daphnis and Pan). Born in the morning, he had invented the lyre before noon, and by nightfall had enticed a herd of fifty away from his duller brother Apollo. May this be an omen of our own powers of lure, for we can find room for three times as many. All this knowing well that the god escorts men through adventures, and protects them in enterprises, and dances whispering prudent counsel in their ear.' At that time I did not know that mercury and quicksilver are the same thing; and Ashley did not know that my nurse called me Quicksilver. It was just a happy coincidence.

Some years later Ashley received a cable from Orson Welles who wanted to name a new American theatre the Mercury and asking Ashley's permission to do so. Of course Ashley said yes.

In the early 1930s I wanted to call our company the Mercury Ballet and managed to do one television performance under that name. But when we were offered a four-week season at the Duke of York's Theatre in 1934, the management insisted on me calling it Ballet Rambert. Ashley in any case was in favour of this – and so it has remained.

At first we planned to do ballet seasons of two weeks each quarter but soon found it impossible, because so many artists had left us. Ashley and I could only provide out of our own means the theatre and the productions. So we limited our performances to Sunday nights only.

In 1933 Ashton was invited to New York to produce the Gertrude Stein-Virgil Thomson *Four Saints in Three Acts*. He made a great impression with it, and that was the beginning of his international fame. On his return I went with his mother to meet him. We felt elated by his success but he himself was very modest about it. However, we laughed a lot in the old shaking taxi.

His next ballet for us was *Mephisto Valse* to Liszt's music of that name. Again the setting and costumes were by Sophie Fedorovitch. She always had a very restrained colour scheme and beautiful designs for costumes – and always enhanced the choreography. Her deep understanding of Ashton was invaluable to him.

He wrote *Mephisto Valse* for Markova, and it was later taken over by Kyra, Nijinsky's daughter. She had offered to join our company – to my amazement and delight – and told me she had danced her father's role in *Spectre de la Rose*. She resembled him very much, but I preferred her to dance the girl in that ballet, and she did it beautifully. As Marguerite, she was deeply touching, and her dancing was exquisite.

She also danced the Mortal born under Neptune in Tudor's *Planets*. He chose three of Holst's *Planets*: Venus, Mars and Neptune – later he added Mercury. He tried out his first ideas for the movements in this ballet with my children on the beach at Dymchurch, and it was after looking at the waves breaking on the shore that he invented the basic movements for Neptune.

His plan was excellent: in each section there was the Planet and the Mortal born under that planet, and satellites to provide more movement. (Astronomy was thrown to the winds.)

There were two Mortals born under Venus, a boy and a girl. The movement of the stars made them meet and part, then meet again a little closer and part, and so on till the end when they are in each other's arms.

In *Mars* the Mortal born under that planet is destined always to fight – in the end he destroys himself. That part was created by Hugh Laing, a strikingly handsome boy, who well expressed the tragic nature of the Mortal born under Mars.

The Mortal born under Neptune is a mystic, longing to unite herself with the Infinite. That part was written for Kyra Nijinsky, and she was absolutely right for it. *The Planets* had wonderful décors and costumes by Hugh Stevenson, possibly his best.

Lysistrata, on Aristophanes' theme, was suggested to Tudor by Ashley (who also hit upon the sub-title *The Strike of Wives*). Tudor chose three pieces of Prokofiev for it. One of the best moments was when Lysistrata, danced very convincingly by Diana Gould, called upon the wives to strike against their husbands. That was followed by a long *pas de deux* for Myrrhina (Markova) and Gore. The choreography had real comedy, but the sonata to which it was danced was quite unsuitable, though beautiful in itself. Prokofiev, who was then in London, came to see it and did not hide his disappointment.

In 1933 Tudor wrote *Atalanta of the East*. He liked the legend but did not feel inclined to use a Greek setting, so he transposed it to the East. There was much beauty in that ballet: the opening in the garden of Hesperides with three goddesses swaying in an exquisite group and yet somehow suggesting the immobility of statues; the entrance of Laing begging for the apple to help him outdo Atalanta in the race; and the race itself. But the rest was very dull, and the music was a poor arrangement of vaguely Eastern tunes which only underlined the weak passages. However, the great beauty of Pearl Argyle in her Eastern make-up, in which she looked a real Nefertiti, and the wonderful appearance of Hugh Laing

compensated a lot for the drawbacks. But after a few performances we dropped that ballet – though I was sorry to lose the
few really inspired moments in it and the décor and costumes
by William Chappell.

In 1933 I went to Paris because Edward James, who was
then founding the 'Ballets 1933' for his wife Tilly Losch, had
engaged four of my pupils for his company. They went to
Kchessinska's classes, and I once went to watch them being
taught by her.

Kchessinska had been the Tsar's mistress, and Lydia
Kyasht had told us how she used to invite a few of the younger
dancers to lunch with her. Then she would say, 'Now what
would you like to see today? Bracelets? Necklaces? Ear-
rings?' And she would pull out a drawer of whatever they
chose. It was a wonderful lesson for the youngsters' morals!

After the Revolution Kchessinska fled abroad, of course; and
she managed to take an enormous fortune with her. But she lost
it at the gambling tables of Monte Carlo. By this time she had
married the Grand Duke Andrei. He used to sweep out the
studio on Sundays and open the door for visitors.

While I was watching her class in Paris, quite entranced
by the splendid work she was doing, the door-bell rang.

'Andrei,' she called out to the Grand Duke. 'Go and open
the door.'

Then she came and whispered in my ear, 'It is the Grand
Duchess Xenia. But please don't go away. I'm not interested
in what she has to say – I know it already – but I do want to
know what you think of my class.'

And she was as happy here in a small hired studio, with the
Grand Duke answering the door, and as absorbed in her class
and her dancing as she had been when she was the virtual
Empress of Russia.

In 1934 a friend of mine, Lesley Blanch, who had been a
great friend of Komisarjevsky and spoke Russian, suggested

that I should go to Russia with her and a group of people organised by the British Drama League. As I spoke Russian they thought I would be useful.

We went on a boat called the *Sibir* (*Siberia*), which was indeed rather grim, being terribly uncomfortable and cramped. But the food was wonderful, and we had caviar for breakfast. After five or six days of this we arrived at Leningrad in the evening. Lesley and I had dinner ashore, and then we went for a walk. I wanted to find Pushkin's house. I knew the name of the street where it was, Moyka. But I did not know how to find the way there, so I asked a workman in Russian, 'Could you tell us the way to Pushkin's house?'

'Oh, yes,' he replied, 'but it's rather complicated. As a matter of fact I've finished my work and am just out for a walk. If you like I'll show you the way.'

So he took us there, and besides looking at the outside of Pushkin's house we walked and talked until two o'clock in the morning. He was a student of agronomy and he told us that his father was a peasant. We asked him how he lived, for we had heard of terrible housing shortages in Russia.

'I'm not badly off,' he said. 'I have part of a room for my wife and myself. And when it comes to doing my studies there are communal work rooms with large tables and good lights. It is all made easy for us.'

The idea of having a house of one's own was almost unthinkable. Once when we were being shown round by an interpreter we passed Prokhorov's house, and she kept repeating, 'It was his *own property*', as though we would not understand what this meant! We spent only one day in Leningrad and then went on to Moscow.

The group from the British Drama League distrusted everything they were shown and told. They were suspicious when people spoke Russian to Lesley and me, and I tried to persuade them they were wrong.

Once we went to a children's theatre to see a play about a

little Negro, called *The Little Black Boy*. We got to the theatre early, and in the foyer there were a lot of children in the charge of a very gay young teacher. She can't have been more than eighteen years old. They were playing a game guessing the names of animals. And I listened to them and tried to guess the clues that she gave to the five-year-olds. Then she described an animal that lived in a very dark place and hardly ever came out. It was almost blind and very black, and so on. But none of the children could guess, until one little voice suddenly said, 'krot' – which means 'mole'.

Then everybody clapped, and the little girl who had guessed right burst into tears, because nobody had ever clapped her before. And I turned to our group and said, 'There you are. You see, *that* wasn't prepared for our benefit!'

In the interval of the play I felt I must get some fresh air because it was so very hot. So I went upstairs and out on to a balcony which looked out over the city. Presently several boys came out too, pushing their way past the other members of the audience. I said to one of them, 'Do you want to stand here?' but he just pushed past me to the balcony rail without answering. Then after a minute or two a teacher came out, very agitated, and pulled the boy back and took him away.

'What's the matter?' I asked the other boys, for I thought that perhaps I had done something wrong.

'He spits on the passers-by.'

This, too, was not prepared for our benefit.

The play itself was charming and beautifully done. We also went to the ballet at the Bolshoi and saw Semenova dance *Swan Lake* quite magnificently. But what struck me most was the extraordinary contrast between the grand scenery, marvellous lighting and superb costumes on the stage, and the people in their shabby working clothes in the auditorium. At the end of the performance Semenova was greeted as in the heyday of the Tsars. There were shouts and people threw their caps in the air.

As guests we sat in what had been the Tsar's box. The

crown and letters 'H II' had been removed and the hammer and sickle had been put in their place, but otherwise the whole plush and gilt theatre was the same as it had always been.

I went several times to the ballet school and I saw Chekrigin give a really marvellous lesson to his dancers. But most of them looked rather fat and they were all dressed in very shabby practice clothes, for there were no good clothes to be had in Russia at all at that time.

I asked Chekrigin why they were so fat, and he said, 'They only eat starchy food. We haven't got enough meat yet.' And he explained that they might have nothing but starch, and perhaps a herring two or three times a week.

I also asked him about their repertory of ballets, which seemed terribly old-fashioned. I had seen marvellous productions by Tairov of new plays. How was it that they were so advanced in the production of drama – yet they stuck so much to the old ballets?

'Give us time,' he said. 'We can only do one thing at a time. First we work at drama. Then we'll work at ballet.'

In 1934 we were offered a season at the Duke of York's Theatre and it proved very successful. The Duke and Duchess of York (King George VI, as he became, and the present Queen Mother) came to one of our performances. I was formally presented to them in their box. Much to our surprise they came again on the Friday of the same week. This time they were sitting in the stalls with Lord Hambleden, whom I knew. He asked me to sit next to him. When the Duchess addressed a question to me, he sprang up to give me his seat and I nearly sat on the royal hand that was holding the seat down for me. This little gesture touched me deeply. Later in the evening there was an unexpected delay while we waited for Ashton. At that time he was dancing at the Saville as well – he had to make money as his salary with us was so small. He was due to be with us for the last ballet, but telephoned to say that he would be late. It was necessary for me to make an announcement from the stage, but I had to confess to Lord Hambleden that I did not know the etiquette. I only knew that I could not start, as I usually did, by saying 'Ladies and Gentlemen.' Thereupon Her Royal Highness, with real concern, said: 'I am so sorry. It is *we* who cause you all this trouble.' What unique graciousness!

I was once at a party given for the present Queen by the British Embassy in Rome. The crowd of guests were surging close around her. Knowing that nobody would notice it, I bent down, picked up the hem of her dress and pressed against my cheek in wonder and delight, just as I had taught the numerous Giselles who had passed through my hands.

For this season at the Duke of York's Ashton wrote *Valentine's Eve* to Ravel's *Valses nobles et sentimentales*. He invented a charming sentimental synopsis. At a ball a young man gives his heart to a girl – symbolised by a heart-shaped ornament on a ribbon. In the next dance she passes it on to her partner who passes it to a girl, and so on, till it returns, to his dismay, to the true lover and breaks his heart.

Sophie designed one of her most perfect sets and costumes – she used only two colours: pink and mulberry. There were screens in mulberry-coloured gauze, and the men's suits were also in that colour, while the girls were in various shades of pink with different ornaments in the hair or round the waist, also in mulberry. The effect of the whole was very original and beautiful. The ballet itself, however, was not so. Somehow Ravel's music in this ballet did not inspire Ashton to his best.

That same year he did his last work for us as he had joined the Sadler's Wells company. It was the *Passionate Pavane* to Dowland's *Lachrimae*, a new version of a little ballet he had written for Lydia Lopokova the previous year for her recitals, and she very generously presented us with the costumes both for that and for another little suite of dances to Boyce's music (to which Frank Staff later wrote his gay *Tartans*).

We had in the company a very young dancer who strikingly resembled the barmaid in Manet's *Bar aux Folies-Bergère*. Her name was Elisabeth Schooling. Ashley used to chuck her under the chin whenever he passed her and say, 'There goes Manet's "Fille au Bar".'

He suggested a ballet on that subject, bringing in the can-can dancers. The waiter, Valentin le Désossé, is in love with the barmaid. He entices her to come out from behind the bar and they dance their love. She returns behind the bar when the can-can dancers appear. They come in through the auditorium (as was the custom in the real Folies-Bergère). The waiter falls for La Goulue and breaks the heart of the barmaid, who resumes her original pose of Manet's painting with which the ballet opened. The music was by Chabrier, chosen by Constant Lambert, and it could not have been better. I remember reading somewhere that Chabrier used to buy his friend Manet's pictures to help him out when there was no demand for them.

Ninette de Valois, whom I asked to compose this ballet for us, made a great success of it. She insisted on Pearl Argyle taking the main role as she was more experienced, but Schooling took it over later, and was most convincing. The dance of the waiter with the barmaid was touchingly simple. Markova's can-can on points was very piquant and wittily danced. The other characters brought much gaiety to that ballet, which remained in our repertoire for twenty years or so.

De Valois and I, by the way, were often taken for each other, although she was much younger and had much better features. She told me she was often addressed as Madame Rambert, and many times people addressed me by her name. Once when she and I were talking during an interval in the stalls, a friend sitting with Ashley in the circle said to him, 'Look at them both now and you will see why they are taken for each other.' Ashley looked down and with a touch of mockery said, 'Professional deformation.'

By this time Ashley was boasting that he was the President (and sole member) of the Society of English Balletophobes. Before he met me he had followed the ballet closely with interest and understanding, and he knew Diaghilev's work well. He always supported me in all my projects and was interested in my early productions. He realised that I had a passion for my work – though he never told me so. It was only in his book that he acknowledged, in his usual restrained fashion, that 'our enterprise was of course entirely dependent on the artistic direction and integrity of Marie Rambert, who undertook complete responsibility back-stage as I undertook it in front.'

But when our daughters began to study ballet, and ballet became the sole topic of conversation at meals, he began to feel that he had had enough of it. I got used to it all and bore it all gaily.

My daughters often became impatient with me, as I seemed to continue the lesson on our way home after class. One day I said to one of them: 'Why did you have such a low arabesque at the end of the last exercise?'

'I was dead tired, after that very hard class.'

'Rubbish. *I* am not tired.'

'Mummy, don't you know that you are a *horse*?'

Even when I felt tired I couldn't stop working. The boys in class also often wilted. I came once into their dressing-room before a rehearsal and said: 'Oh, I feel so tired, I had such a bad night. If only I could sleep what energy I should have!'

In one voice they all exclaimed: 'God forbid that you should ever sleep!'

In addition to Ashton and Tudor we had a group of choreographers who appeared from our ranks in those early days. Andrée Howard, after seven years in my school, had been engaged in 1933 by de Basil, who had just started his company in Monte Carlo. There she had suddenly decided, after six months, that she did not want to dance and wished only to be a choreographer. She returned to me and asked to be allowed to try her hand in a new version of *Our Lady's Juggler*, originally written by Susan Salaman. It proved an excellent ballet, and we kept it in our repertoire for a long time. Her second ballet, *The Mermaid*, was deeply poetic. It was done to Ravel's *Allegro for Harp and Strings*, and it followed the story of Hans Andersen's *Little Mermaid*.

Andrée's imaginative use of the stage did wonders. We first saw the little mermaid playing with her sisters among seaweed at the bottom of the sea. The seaweed was made of long strips of gauze hanging from the flies at the back of the stage, and in front there was a gauze curtain of the same sea-green colour, all beautifully lit. The costumes and movements designed by Andrée perfectly suggested the sea creatures.

The second scene was on the surface of the sea, and we saw a boat represented just by one large sail, with the prince leaning against the mast and the other sailors lying or sitting on the deck (the floor of the stage) in the sun. But the wind rises and they stand up anxiously. The music becomes more stormy and the prince calls upon them to take to the oars. Now the storm breaks out, the boat is tossed about and they all drown.

The third scene was again like the first, the bottom of the sea. The prince sinks towards it, the little mermaid falls in love with him and saves him by lifting him up to the surface. But now she wants to follow him and calls on magic to change her fish-tail into human legs.

The fourth scene is on a terrace by the sea. The prince dances with his earthly bride and friends. The music here was the *Alborada del gracioso* of Ravel. An uncanny motive creeps into the music – they all sense something strange. The mermaid emerges from the sea, but the very first steps on land cause her terrible pain. She knew that this pain was the condition on which she could obtain the change into a woman, and also that if she failed to win the prince's love she would go back to the sea, not any more as a mermaid but as mere foam. She risked all, and lost her prince to his earthly bride.

Pearl Argyle was incredibly beautiful and moving in that role and one can hardly believe how convincing all those changes of scenery were, and how imaginative. The French poet Jean-Louis Vaudoyer (who had suggested to Diaghilev the theme of *Spectre de la Rose* from Gautier's poem), saw our *Mermaid* at the Mercury and wrote: 'Quand elle danse, Miss Pearl Argyle enchante les yeux, mais elle fait aussi battre les cœurs, et nous nous souvenons de l'émotion unanime qu'éprouva la salle, lorsque, surgie des eaux et devenue par amour une femme mortelle, la Petite Sirène toucha pour la première fois la terre de ses pieds nouveau-nés.'

Paul Valéry also saw Pearl as the mermaid and said profound and exquisite words to her. Her great probity of nature, her intelligence and wit made her the ideal instrument for a great variety of roles.

The following year Andrée did an excellent comic ballet, *La Muse s'Amuse*, but unfortunately the music of Déodat de Séverac did not support the mood of comedy.

Her masterpiece came in 1939 when she composed *Lady into Fox* from David Garnett's novel, to music of Honegger. Nadia Benois designed the perfect scenery and costumes, and the change from the woman into the fox was done in a few seconds – a thrilling moment. She solved the problem of transforming an Edwardian lady into a fox on the stage most brilliantly. Inside the bustle of the dress was a pocket in which was fitted the fox's tail. The costume was reddish brown towelling with a beautiful red wig dressed so that it looked like a fox's head with pricked up ears. Between them was placed what is called a 'bang', a sort of curly fringe. When the dancer was transformed, dress and bang were pulled off quickly to reveal her as a fox.

This was the real début of Sally Gilmour, though she had already danced small roles before. Her fox was indeed an un-

53. My original company
Prudence Hyman, Ashton, Tudor, Markova, Andrée Howard, Rambert, Robert Stuart, Pearl Argyle, Diana Gould, Maude Lloyd, Elisabeth Schooling, Betty Cuff; *on the ground:* Chappell, Doone, Suzette Morfield

54. The company today
Joseph Scoglio, Graham Jones, Jeremy Allen, Gideon Avrahami, Sylvia Byrne, Dreas Reyneke, Lucy Burge, Christopher Bruce, Norman Morrice, Peter Curtis, Rambert, Nicoline Nystrom, John Chesworth, Marilyn Williams, Jonathan Taylor, Paul Taras, Sally Owen, Julia Blackie (*halfway*), Susan Cooper, Amanda Knott, Mary Willis, Sandra Craig, Mary Prestidge

55. Curtain call after *Paris-Soir* by Gore, showing the minute size of the stage at the Mercury

56. Ashley and myself at the entrance to the Mercury Theatre

57. Our Theatre

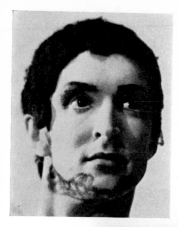

58. Antony Tudor

59. Tudor's *The Planets: Venus* with Pearl Argyle and Chappell

60. (*bottom left*) *Neptune* with Antony Tudor and Kyra Nijinska

61. *Jardin aux Lilas,* original cast and costumes, Laing, Peggy van Praagh, Tudor, Maude Lloyd

62. Last moment in *Jardin aux Lilas*

63. At the dress rehearsal of *Dark Elegies*

64. *Dark Elegies:* Tudor, Lloyd, van Praagh, de Mille, Gore

65. (*top left*) Andrée Howard in *Pompette*. She made the costume and Ashton composed a dance for it

66. (*top right*) *Our Lady's Juggler*, Rambert and Harold Turner

67. (*left*) Pearl Argyle as the Mermaid

68. Maude Lloyd in *Mermaid*, my daughter Helena second from the left, and Angela second from the right

69. *Cinderella*, Argyle and Ashton; note the glamour of décor and costumes on that tiny stage

70. *Lady into Fox:* Charles Boyd and Sally Gilmour

71. Sally Gilmour as Tulip in *The Sailor's Return*

72. *The Tartans*: Frank Staff, Elisabeth
Schooling, Anthony Kelly

73. Lulu Dukes in *Peter and the Wolf*

74. Gore and Gilmour as Mr
Punch and Polly

75. Walter Gore

76. *Giselle*, end of Act I

77. Belinda Wright and John Gilpin, Australia 1947

tamed creature and one longed for her to escape into the forest
away from the tender love of her husband and devoted nurse.
Sally was an outstanding artist.

Tudor wrote *Jardin aux Lilas* in 1936. The subject was
suggested to him by Hugh Stevenson, who did a perfect,
though obvious, setting of clumps of lilac bushes and beautiful
costumes, very expressive of the various characters. Here is
the synopsis as printed in the programme.

Caroline, on the eve of her marriage to the man she does
not love, tries to say farewell to her lover at a garden reception, but is constantly interrupted by guests and in the end
goes off on the arm of her betrothed with hopelessness in her
eyes. The situation is complicated by the presence of her
betrothed's former love.

The interplay of feelings between these characters was
revealed in beautiful dance movements and groupings, with
subtle changes of expression, which made each situation clear
without any recourse to mime or gesture. It could be called a
'ballet psychologique' on the same ground as Stendhal's
'roman psychologique'. It had one quite startling moment:
at the height of the drama the movement froze and the music
continued alone for several bars. It made you hold your
breath. The whole ballet was perfect and has become a classic.
Although it had been composed on the small stage of the
Mercury it bore transference to the Metropolitan Opera
House in New York. In fact, as I have indicated, those of our
Mercury ballets that were good became even better on big
stages, because the dancers could take wing after the restricted
space of our own stage – and the integrity of the work itself
shone the brighter.

Should I have abstained from describing in such detail so
many of our ballets? I know full well how little my words can
convey, without the dancing, the music and the décor. But
there was poetry in them, and they were the first-born of our
repertoire.

We now began to have seasons outside London. In 1936 we had a fortnight at Barry Jackson's Repertory Theatre in Birmingham, which was followed by yearly seasons at the same theatre and later at the Alexandra.

During one of these seasons at Birmingham a friend of mine brought Sir Walter Monckton and a distinguished judge to see our performance. They enjoyed the show very much and when it was over they wanted to offer me some entertainment in return.

'Tomorrow', they said, 'we are going to hear the case of the Indian doctor who has been accused of indecently assaulting a patient. Would you like to come? It might amuse you.'

This case had been in all the papers and had made a tremendous noise in London. Ashley told me that in the Garrick it was known as the 'Indian Rape Trick'.

So next day I went, and to my staggered surprise was made to sit on the Bench with the judge and my other two friends. The prosecuting counsel was not content with asking the doctor to describe what he had done, he made him demonstrate it in front of us all. It was appalling. I felt so ashamed. My face was burning as though I was myself accusing him of all these indecencies. I never knew until then that shame can be as painful as terror.

I couldn't wait for it to finish. At last they announced the adjournment for lunch, and as we went out someone started telling me what time to come back. 'No fear,' I said. 'You'll never see me again,' and I fled.

In 1937 we were offered a tour in France, taking in all the great resorts like Vichy (on the very stage where Diaghilev's company had given its last performance), Deauville, La Baule and others. I wanted to take my daughters with me, as they were by now beginning to dance in our ballets, but Ashley opposed the tour vehemently. The impresario concerned was a woman whom he did not trust. He described her as 'seedy, shifty, shady'.

'Furthermore,' he said, 'I am not going to have my daughters leered at by square-bearded Frenchmen!'

This virulent expostulation made me roar with laughter – he was the last person to speak like a Colonel Blimp. Besides, he loved France, was a French scholar and had translated several French plays. He had even talked of founding a 'Société pour débaucher les camemberts trop vierges'.

I won my battle with Ashley, but he won the point about the daughters. The tour proved very exciting, as most of the company had never been abroad. We took thirty ballets, of which the ones that pleased most were *Foyer de Danse, Bar aux Folies-Bergère* and *Death and the Maiden* – a beautiful short ballet by Andrée Howard to Schubert's music. In one of the towns we ran out of programmes, and the management insisted that one of their staff should announce the ballets. She was a coarse creature and her voice jarred on me each time she pronounced the name of one of our ballets. She omitted to announce *Death and the Maiden* in time, and so had to do it when the ballet was over. But by then she was completely transformed. Deeply moved, with a voice broken by tears, she said. 'This very beautiful thing you have just seen is *Death and the Maiden*'.

I made friends with her after that. But Ashley's warning was right, and we were cheated of our earnings by the seedy-shifty-shady lady.

On our return from that tour we had a season at the Duchess Theatre. Tudor told me he was anxious to do a ballet to Mahler's *Kindertotenlieder* (Songs on the death of children).

He had already suggested it two years before, but at that time I did not think he was mature enough to tackle such a tragic subject. I had also been perturbed by the main idea of a disaster that would kill all the children and leave the parents alive. I kept reasoning with Tudor that except for the Massacre of the Innocents such a special calamity had never happened and would seem *too* contrived. But now in 1937 he seemed very sure of the way to treat it. I asked him to show me one finished song and realised how profound the choreography was. He had seen at an exhibition of Nadia Benois a landscape which he was sure would be the right setting, and when I saw the painting I agreed with him. So we invited her to design the scenery and the costumes, which she did perfectly. The ballet was not purely realistic. It had lovely words and music, and the dances were classical for the soloists and in folk-dance style for the ensemble. Yet he managed to keep the style homogeneous.

He called this ballet *Dark Elegies*. It was in two scenes: 1: Bereavement; 2: Resignation. It was like a mourning ritual accompanied by a singer on the stage. Singly or in groups, the bereaved parents express their sorrow in a slow dance at having lost their children when their village was stricken by calamity. They try not to show their pain, but it breaks through at moments. All was said in classical language, and this severe form made the expression more poignant when despair burst through it.

When we performed this ballet in 1966 to a new young public, many of them thought that it was all about the Aberfan Disaster, to such a degree had the most unforeseen of calamities happened in reality.

Dark Elegies was Tudor's masterpiece and has remained the greatest tragic ballet of the English repertoire so far.

In addition to our own dancers he used a guest dancer, the American Agnes de Mille, a most remarkable artist. She used to come to my classes whenever she was in London, and we

became great friends. I admired her as dancer and choreographer as well as writer. In her book *Dance to the Piper* she
drew a very lively portrait of me, describing my lesson in her
own humorous way. But she was sorry I did not have 'the
iron trap-like intention to force success'.

In 1937 Tudor left me to found his own company, which he
called the London Ballet. It gave performances at Toynbee
Hall on Mondays, following our Sunday ones. The four principals were ex-members of the Ballet Rambert and continued
to dance the parts in ballets that had been created for them at
the Mercury. Maude Lloyd was the only one who continued
to dance both with us and with them. For the London Ballet
Tudor composed *Gala Performance* to Prokofiev's Classical
Symphony, *Soirée Musicale* to Rossini-Britten, and *Judgement
of Paris* to Kurt Weill. The London Ballet rejoined my company in 1940, and we took over all these ballets as well as the
beautiful *Fête Etrange* by Andrée Howard, to Fauré's music
and designs by Sophie Fedorovitch.

Later that ballet was taken over by the Royal Ballet and
looked even more beautiful on the stage of Covent Garden.

Walter Gore, who came to me in 1930, was a brilliant
dancer. His first attempt at choreography was *Valse Finale*
using Sophie Fedorovitch sets for *Valentine's Eve* and Ravel's
music. It showed talent, but was not a good ballet – and that
was also the case with his next ballet *Paris-Soir*. It was only
after the war that he proved his importance as choreographer.

Frank Staff wrote an amusing little ballet called *The Tartans*
to music by Boyce in 1938. It was a new version of a ballet
Ashton had arranged for Lopokova in 1930, and was a series
of dances for three people: Elisabeth Schooling was very fetch-
ing in her Scots Grey hat and kilt, with Staff and Gore as her
partners – a most delicious suite of dances.

Many members of our company, especially men, had to earn
their living at Sadler's Wells, and so we could only have
performances on Sunday evenings.

It had long been Ashley's desire to put on seasons of plays by poets. The moment for this was propitious, and so he began performances on weekdays. The first was W. J. Turner's *Jupiter Translated,* for which Nadia Benois did a beautiful back-cloth representing the Horses of the Night (which was later used for the ballet, *The Descent of Hebe*). This was how she first came to our theatre. Later, as I have recounted, her lovely designs for *Lady into Fox* also contributed much to the early success of the theatre.

Among the many plays presented by Ashley was T. S. Eliot's *Murder in the Cathedral,* produced by E. Martin Browne, which ran for over 200 nights – a record for our Mercury. Later we also had W. H. Auden and Isherwood's *The Ascent of F6,* Synge's *The Playboy of the Western World* (with Cyril Cusack as Christy Mahon and Maire O'Neill as the Widow Quin) – but it would take many chapters to write about Ashley's productions.

The actors made great friends with our dancers, in spite of little quarrels over rehearsal rooms. There used to be lively arguments when the rehearsal schedule was put up on the board. I remember hearing someone say: 'There seems to be no room anywhere, what with *Murder* in the upper studio and *Rape* in the basement.' (*Murder in the Cathedral* happened to coincide with Andrée Howard's ballet, *The Rape of the Lock.*)

During the run of *Murder in the Cathedral,* T. S. Eliot often came to the performances, and afterwards there were always people talking with him in the bar. I asked him once what he thought was the greatest novel in the world. I hoped he would say *War and Peace,* and, to my joy, he did. I then asked him what he would consider the second. He thought a while and said: '*Anna Karenina*?' He paused again and added: 'Or is it *David Copperfield*?' After that I asked each of the others there and I think all agreed about *War and Peace* being the greatest. But when it came to the next best, opinions differed a great deal. Someone said *Madame Bovary,* someone else *Chartreuse*

de Parme, some said *Vanity Fair,* others *Pride and Prejudice.*
But no two persons could agree.

One night Ashley took a box to see Edwige Feuillière and
invited Eliot and John Hayward to come with us. In the interval I saw Markova in the stalls and asked Eliot whether he
would like to meet her. When I brought her up, I said, 'Here
is the Taglioni of today.' Thereupon Hayward said, 'You
should rather say "Markova of today".' But Eliot topped it by
saying, 'No, what one should say is "Taglioni was the
Markova of *her* day".'

Once in a taxi with Eliot, I casually recited 'Growltiger'.
He was so pleased that the next day he sent me his Possum
book of cats, signed 'Old Possum'.

In August 1939 we went to dance in Dublin – a city I loved
at first sight, and have loved ever since. It always reminds me
of Moscow at the beginning of this century: the same character of buildings, the way it lies on the Liffey, and the peculiar
charm of its inhabitants.

On this visit I arrived late at Dublin railway station, and
was in a frantic hurry wondering whether I was on time. I
looked for a clock and saw that it said two o'clock. I might be
on time after all. Then I saw another clock which said two-
fifteen. Bewildered and outraged I rushed up to a porter.

'What do you mean by it?' I protested. 'Here you have
two clocks showing different times.'

'Fwhat would be the use, miss,' he replied, 'of having two
clocks if they both showed the same time?'

In Ireland, of course, we had to play the Irish National
Anthem. But I wanted to play 'God Save the King' too. I
suggested to the theatre manager that perhaps we could have
one anthem at the beginning and the other at the end. But he
made difficulties about it.

'Well, 'I suggested, 'suppose we just play the first half.'

'What do you mean "the first half"?'

'Well,' I said. 'Just "God save our . . ."'

But before I could get any further he said, 'Stop it, dammit!'

Even to mention 'our glorious King' seemed a blasphemy in Republican Ireland.

After Dublin the company dispersed for holidays, and we went for ours to Perranporth in Cornwall. There was a small Summer Theatre run by Peter Bull, in which excellent plays were presented with remarkable casts. Among them were young Pamela Brown, Robert Morley and Hermione Gingold, whom I knew because she had recently appeared at the Mercury in Ashley's presentation of a play by Jean Jacques Bernard.

We used to meet in the mornings for the deliciously exciting surf-riding and had carefree days until that fateful Sunday when we heard Neville Chamberlain announce the war. That, of course, seemed to be the end of everything. We all thought that London would be wiped out at once, and with so many called up there seemed no prospect of any stage work.

I was bombarded with telegrams and letters from my pupils' parents begging me to find a place in the country where I could continue my school. My good friends the Louis Behrends let me have a part of their lovely Gray House at Burghclere near Newbury. It was they, by the way, who had built and endowed that chapel in Burghclere completely covered with beautiful frescoes by Stanley Spencer.

We were lucky to find within a mile of us a school that had been evacuated from London and could provide general education for our pupils. They cycled there every morning after their first dancing lesson in the studio at Gray House. Unfortunately nobody was there to teach French, as the teacher had left to join her family – so I was prevailed upon to undertake it. This I did in the most unorthodox way: first we learnt to sing the *Marseillaise* with a record – the rousing tune helped the children to remember the words and the perfect pronunciation was underlined by it. Then I dictated it, telling them how to spell it and translate it. It was so successful that soon we learnt some more songs, this time by Charles Trenet.

Our lessons were very gay, and within two terms French became quite familiar to them.

Altogether it was an amusing interlude. One day when I was sitting in a field, I overheard a conversation between two little Cockney evacuees. One said to the other: 'You see that black cow over there? I bet you he gives black milk.'

But when Easter came and the phoney war seemed to be continuing, I decided to return with the school to London.

THE COMPANY also reassembled in London, and we decided, in spite of the blackout, to accept the offer of a season at the Duchess Theatre, where Frank Staff produced his *Czernyana*. It was a series of Czerny's piano exercises, so well chosen and choreographed that it formed a complete ballet, much enhanced by the décor and costumes of Eve Swinstead-Smith. Some of the pieces were satirical and very witty, like *Se habla español*, *Visions*, *Trop Symphonique*, *Presque Classique*; some romantic like *Les Belles Somnolentes* and *Nuages* – the last two with very original movement and grouping, and the whole ballet finished with an exciting gallop in masks.

We also tried to continue our Sundays at the Mercury, but with the call-up of our men it became increasingly difficult – and so, very reluctantly, I consented to join a new organisation, The Arts Theatre Club in Leicester Square. Ashley was very opposed to my joining that organisation, which was run by a very rich man. He kept repeating, 'Don't have anything to do with somebody who has only money to recommend him.' But I was losing my artists and could not see how to save my company.

The director was a very ambitious man and wished to make it a 'Centre of Ballet'. He had in addition to us two other companies dancing there, one of which was Tudor's London Ballet, which was then being run by Maude Lloyd and Peggy Van Praagh, as Tudor had joined the Ballet Theatre in America.

At that time Myra Hess had the brilliant idea of giving lunchtime concerts at the National Gallery. We copied her example and began to give lunchtime ballet at the Arts Theatre. Air-raid wardens and night workers of all sorts used to come and have a snack lunch and then an hour of ballet, after which, properly relaxed from the strain of their restless night, they could go to sleep for a few hours. It became so popular that we also did tea-time performances, and then as many as four performances a day.

The three companies used to take turns in touring dates. Our first date was in Cambridge at the Arts Theatre, for which Frank Staff produced a very amusing ballet on Prokofiev's *Peter and the Wolf*. My daughter Lulu had her first real part as Peter. Sally Gilmour was the enchanting Duck and Celia Franca a brilliant Bird. The rest of the cast was excellent too, and the setting and costumes by Guy Sheppard framed it all perfectly. The audiences laughed a great deal and felt happy for an hour. We were always surprised to get good houses, as the black-out made theatre-going very difficult. Also, with the air-raids, some streets were made impassable overnight and one never knew who would manage to get to a rehearsal. At the bombing of the Café de Paris one of my dancers, Prudence Hyman, lay pinned for two hours under a block of cement before she could be released. She was stitched up and after six weeks danced again as brilliantly as ever.

One night in Cambridge as I was walking to my digs, an American soldier followed me whispering silly endearments. I stopped right under a lamp so that he could see my face and said:

'Aren't you a fool, you see I could be your mother – but I would *not*!'

There was quite a new public coming to see ballet, as we carried it to war-workers, canteens, soldiers' camps, airfields, factories and so on, as well as to the big theatres. I often went in the interval to the bar to listen to them. One evening an American soldier stayed on after the bell had called the audience back. He went up to the barmaid, pointed to a poster of next week's show and asked in a pitiful voice: 'Say, miss, do they *talk*?'

Poor man, he must have been bored stiff seeing all this lot of pretty girls never uttering a word.

The enterprise at the Arts Theatre in Leicester Square came to an end in 1941, and for a whole year after that we were debarred by legal difficulties from giving performances. But in 1943 the newly-formed C.E.M.A. (Council for the Encouragement of Music and the Arts, which later developed into the Arts Council) took us under their wing. We started with a small company of eleven, for which Andrée Howard wrote her amusing *Carnival of Animals* (Saint-Saëns). Walter Gore, who was in the Navy, used to come to the studio when on one of his short leaves and work on his new ballet to Benjamin Britten's *Simple Symphony*. It was in four movements aptly named by Britten (1) *Boisterous Bourrée*, (2) *Playful Pizzicato*, (3) *Sentimental Sarabande*, (4) *Frolicsome Finale*, and these moods were perfectly rendered in Gore's choreography.

Once, when we danced for a week at Brockwell Park, we had the unexpected joy of having three of our men on leave at the same time. They found ballet classes much harder than the P.T. in the Army or Navy and, to our amazement, wilted after the barre, in spite of the remarkable vigour of their appearance. Walter had been torpedoed, and rescued, and torpedoed again the same day in the ship that had rescued him. After that he was in hospital till he got demobilised. We became quite used to the bombs and went on with our work, not even troubling to go down to the basement at the alert.

I had a painful experience in 1944 when I returned from Cambridge, where I went once weekly to teach ballet to undergraduates. Liverpool Street station had been bombed. There were firemen hosing the burning roof and the platforms were flooded. I could hardly get out of the station and began to walk in the hopes of finding a taxi. But every street was gutted with rubble, through which I could hardly walk, and there was fire above and water below, and I felt I would never get out of it all. It was really like hell.

It was one of the worst moments of the war for me, except for the day when returning once more from Cambridge, I saw a house sprawling across the road in my street in Notting Hill Gate. For one ghastly moment I thought it was our house, but coming nearer found it was the house opposite ours and another next to it. Ashley was on the threshold, unrecognisable, with rubble encrusted to his face. All the windows had been smashed – my daughter, fortunately, had flung herself under her bed just before the window flew in across it. Five people were killed opposite us, and for a whole year a book-case with several books on one of its shelves remained hanging on a naked wall on the third floor – a most dismal sight.

But in spite of all these horrors we enjoyed dancing to all the new audiences. I often had to give a little introductory talk and it seemed to help them to enjoy their first experience of ballet, and after that many became fans.

Some of them not only greeted us with flowers but brought much more substantial and welcome gifts. One middle-aged couple in Norfolk were particularly generous. They used to bring me eggs, butter and fruit, and once even a chicken. They kept begging me to come and stay with them on their farm. After some time I managed to snatch a week because of some cancellation, so I rang them up and they were delighted. They were cultivated people, had a splendid collection of books, almost all first editions and they were charming to talk to, so I was looking forward to my stay with them. When H. met me at the station he said: 'Do you mind if we lunch in a restaurant, I have quite a bit of shopping to do in town.' I was very disappointed, having made up my mind to eat only farm food. After lunch we went to a grocer's, and I was staggered to see him buy tins of fish, meat, and even vegetables.

We came to the farm at last. On entering the dining-room

I saw the hostess with two live cats round her neck by way of a boa. Her son, a young man, had a live cat hanging from his collar by way of a tie. In addition to that there were two cats sitting cosily on the table and several others on the floor. I counted them while talking to my hosts and found there were fourteen. I counted again (still talking) and there they were – still fourteen. So I could not refrain from saying: 'What a lot of cats, where have you got them from?' 'Oh, this is less than half of what we have,' they said. A shudder shook me. I hate cats and they love me, as cats will.

In order to sit down at the table I had to shake the chair violently to push off the cat. No sooner was I seated than two cats leapt on to my lap. My hosts did not seem to notice any of this, they did not even chase the two cats from the table.

After tea the hostess took me to my room and said: 'Now I hope you'll be comfortable here.' I started unpacking but immediately a cat appeared on the threshold. I chased him in a fury and closed the door. But the door did not close unless you slammed it, a hateful thing to do.

I opened the wardrobe to hang up my clothes, but it was absolutely full. So I thought I could put all my clothes in the chest of drawers – but there was no room there even for a hankie, it was so packed. Then I thought a hook on the door might do, but there was none. I finally threw it all back into my case.

The host prided himself on being a 'Cordon bleu', and indeed the salmon was delicious, but the supper was at ten instead of at eight and the cats ate most of the fish. Then they gave me a box of matches and explained that there was no gas or electricity in the house, but there was an oil lamp and a candle. The lamp was too complicated, so I could not read the two or three hours I always read when sleepless. At last I fell asleep about three. At five o'clock piercing shrieks from a guinea fowl woke me up. How I cursed! I thought of sending a wire to Ashley to say would he wire me that I was urgently needed at home. But the previous day I had just finished a travel book describing extraordinary hardships, I think in Tibet, and I thought that if that young man could put up with all those torments, I must force myself to bear these comparatively small discomforts. Also, I liked my hosts and did not want to cheat them with that wire.

Their greatest interest was their magnificent herd of Jerseys and a fine breed of pigs. They left the house at seven in the morning, and there I was, unable to light a fire and cook anything. So I drank some milk, shielding myself all the time from the cats, and ate bread. After that I wanted to go for a walk. No fear: the goose, Jack, guarded the door and wanted my blood. So I crawled through the back, hoping that by the time I returned Mr and Mrs H. would be back. They were, but there was no lunch till three, and that was only one scrambled egg, mercifully on toast. The explanation of it was that they always had a small breakfast before milking the cows and then a large one at ten, when I was out. I swear to it, it was not premeditated.

The really extraordinary thing was that in spite of all those cats, the house was infested with mice. The cats were not allowed in the larder, and so the mice had a great time of it. They ran about all over the place. One of them had been too adventurous; he had put his head into an open jam jar and got drowned in that. But when I asked why they did not poison them or let the cats loose on them, they were absolutely horrified. They adored all the animals, obviously including vermin.

Yet they were a most unusual pair to talk to, and I loved them in spite of all. Never did I write a word about all of this to Ashley. It was a sort of test I imposed on myself. On the last day, when I was already in the car with Mr and Mrs H., the young H. pulled me out as he was resolved to make me stroke the bull. I was lifted by him over the bull's enclosure and had to put my hands between his horns, trembling all over. The H.s came with me to London to spend a day in our house, and it was only after they had left that I told all this story to Ashley – and wrote it down at once, as I knew that otherwise I would never believe it really had happened to me.

In 1944 we gave a season at the Mercury with several of Tudor's ballets. Nadia Benois had brought some American friends, and one of them assured me that my production of Tudor's ballets was even better than his own in America. I said that though I loved compliments I must first believe them, and that I was sure that Antony's own production must be better than mine because he knew more exactly what he wanted. Besides, he had all the stars.

'He may have all the stars but you have the team-work,' replied Nadia's friend.

Thereupon Nadia's son, Peter Ustinov, said:

'Team-work? You mean Mim-work!'

On another occasion at the dinner of a Music Society at which I was guest of honour, Peter made a very witty speech, and said amongst other things:

'If the custom of the old school tie prevailed among dancers, the best old school tights would be in Rambert's colours.' At the same dinner the chairman of the society asked Peter to give the toast of the Queen. Peter pointed out that the guests were already smoking, but the chairman insisted. So Peter gave the Toast, and as the guests were sitting down again he said: 'Ladies and Gentlemen, you may continue to smoke.'

Peter once told Ashley that he saw him in the Park, being 'led on reins by an extremely small boy' – in fact our two-year-old grandson.

We travelled the length and breadth of England during those war years, dancing on stages of all sizes: one week it could be the Opera House in Manchester, the next an improvised stage in a canteen, where workers hurried with their lunch to see a half-hour performance before resuming their work.

At last came that heavenly day when peace was declared. We all walked with the crowds through the streets singing, and in the evening climbed on to those huge figures round Queen Victoria's statue opposite Buckingham Palace, and clamoured for the King and Queen, who appeared on the balcony, somehow symbolising victory and peace.

And soon we could travel again.

In December 1945 we were sent on a two-month tour of Germany, dancing for our troops in various garrison theatres. We had been lent to E.N.S.A., an organisation of artists specially for troops, and it was most exciting being fitted for our military uniforms and receiving official briefings from senior officers. We had to spend a night in a hostel in Folkestone before embarking early in the morning. We hardly ate any breakfast, saving our appetite to eat a lovely French lunch in Calais. We were issued with sandwiches for the journey but disdained them for the same reason and threw them to the gulls. When we were within a mile of Calais a sudden fog descended, and the ship which should have made room for us there could not leave. We had to drop anchor and sit tight for eighteen hours. There was no food whatever on our ship, the *Royal Daffodil*, and no bunks for the night, as in peace time she was only a cross-Channel steamer. We were all very hungry, bitterly regretting those sandwiches we had thrown light-heartedly to the gulls.

About eleven in the evening a small launch arrived from Calais carrying French loaves, English tea and American spam. We ate and drank the New Year in with this international fare, and stretched ourselves on the floor for the night. In addition to some thirty dancers there were three times as many officers and soldiers. Those who could not find room on the floor fell asleep sitting at tables, poor things. About four in the morning the fog lifted and we landed at Calais. From there we went by coach to Ostend, where we had hot baths and excellent food, and proceeded to Brussels

for the train to Hamburg. That train had no heating whatever, and lots of the windows had been broken by our soldiers
in celebrating their demobilisation. The temperature was
well below freezing, and if one spilt tea from a thermos it at
once froze on the floor. We wore all the clothes we had, plus
our battle dress as well and greatcoats, caps and scarves. We
used our mackintoshes to stop the wind rushing through the
broken windows. After thirty-six hours in that train we at
last arrived in Hamburg at 3 a.m. It was pitch dark. Someone
was calling my name. I thought that they wanted to give me
flowers and was preparing to throw them back at them – but,
oh bliss, they handed me a lovely hot-water bottle.

Hamburg was in ruins. One could walk miles through the
devastation without seeing a human being. But we were put
into the best hotel and were very well looked after. A German
woman who was there offered to give us beauty treatment in
exchange for cigarettes. I asked her what she felt about
Hitler now. With great courage and honesty she said : 'Don't
ask us to hate him, the love we gave him cannot be changed
into hate by order.'

We were wonderfully entertained with parties every night
after the performance, with delicious cakes brought over from
Denmark and other rich food we had forgotten existed.

In Lübeck we met a lot of Russian officers. They gave us
parties on their ship, and we sang and danced with them.
Because I spoke Russian I received more than my share of
attention, in spite of my age. When I said to one of them:
'But can you not see my grey hair ?' he replied with rapture :
'My darling, silvery Madamchik.'

So I became his Silvylocks and he my Goldyteeth (his
teeth proudly exhibited their gold fillings).

We did quite a big tour, the whole way by coach. When
we were on the Autobahn just going into Berlin, I stopped
the coach and started cartwheeling towards the city. Two
girls followed my example and we went three abreast amid

great shouts of laughter – it really was a victorious entry.

We saw the sinister Reichstag and visited the odious (and commodious) shelter where Hitler had lived. We cut bits off his carpet for souvenirs. Sally Gilmour put her foot on Hitler's bed and said: 'This really makes me feel we've won the war.'

Our performances were forbidden to the Germans, but when some of their dancers asked my permission to attend my classes I gave it gladly. Amongst them was the now famous Peter Van Dijk.

It was wonderful to find Ashley in Berlin at his work. He had been appointed Cultural Adviser for Music and Drama with the Control Commission in Berlin. He introduced me to many German theatre people, all eager to start work again, and most appreciative of Ashley's deep understanding of their problems. Altogether he was with the Commission for two years, doing very interesting, and I am sure fruitful, work.

In the summer of 1946 we gave a long season at Sadler's
Wells, for which we produced our first full length classic
Giselle. We had started working on the second act the year
before and produced it separately in Birmingham. We had
beautiful sets and costumes by Hugh Stevenson and, in Sally
Gilmour, a most touching Giselle, with Gore as her perfect
partner. Joyce Graeme, who taught us the Mariinski version,
which she had learnt from Nicolas Sergeev, was a menacing
Queen of the Wilis. I longed to have the swinging branch on
which Giselle first appears in the second act. It was a very
simple device, but it would have cost fifty pounds; we could not
afford it, which gives an idea of how we had to count every penny.

This production was so well received that I decided to produce the first act as well. Sonia Arova was with us as a guest
artist and even in the small part of Bathilda created a
memorable character. It was matched only when the Bolshoi
brought over their famous production. When Arova danced
the Moscow ballerina in Tudor's *Gala Performance*, she was
unsurpassed both in dancing and comedy. The peasant *pas de
deux* in *Giselle* was danced by Belinda Wright and John
Gilpin, who had joined my school some years before, and
were now sixteen years old.

Gore wrote a new ballet for that season, *Mr Punch*, to a
score commissioned from Arthur Oldham – and, incidentally,
warmly recommended by Britten. It was a major work, and
his own role of *Mr Punch* had an epic quality – he painted the
real national character of that famous puppet. Some critics

described it as an English *Petrushka*, but with a gay, not pathetic, character.

Our *Giselle* was very much praised and we felt it raised our status as a company. Although our *corps de ballet* did not have the required number of dancers, the effect it produced was absolutely right. Everybody knows that a work of art does not depend on its size. A quartet of Beethoven may be as great as one of his symphonies. A painting is not valued by the size of its canvas, yet the public idea of a ballet is often a stage covered with a huge *corps de ballet*, especially in the English provinces. I once saw a ballet company advertise '100 dancers', as though that in itself was a guarantee of quality.

Fortunately the romantic ballets do not require a very large *corps de ballet*, and as the patterns of these works are usually symmetrical it is easy to reduce the numbers without affecting the design.

I felt very happy about our *Giselle*, which moved me at each performance, and had the same effect on the audience. When the Bolshoi first came here and we had the revelation of Ulanova, the critics agreed that our production was the nearest in spirit to theirs.

We had an offer to go to Australia in 1947. An impresario who had seen a great deal of ballet came to see us and to my unexpected delight spoke with great enthusiasm of our company. His name was Dan O'Connor. He had only arrived from New Zealand a few days before, but as soon as he saw us he decided it was the right moment to take us to Australia. I asked him when he had seen our performance. He said it was the previous Thursday matinée. I was horrified because it had been an extremely hot day and poor house, but he said that the company had danced as at a great gala and he had judged their quality by their performance. I am forever grateful to him for those words. He offered a contract for a tour of six months (which actually turned into eighteen months).

But before that we had to get ready for our annual London season at Sadler's Wells. Gore had prepared a delightful ballet *Plaisance*, to Rossini's music, which he gave me as a present on the twentieth anniversary of our company, and Andrée Howard was working on *The Sailor's Return*. This had a prologue and two acts, and was the first English ballet of that length. The story was taken from David Garnett's novel of that name, and Arthur Oldham was commissioned to write the music. Andrée herself did the excellent set and costumes.

In the short prologue, which takes place in Dahomey, we saw the pagan wedding of an English sailor with a native girl, Tulip. In the first act there is their arrival at the sailor's village in England and the buying of the inn 'The Sailor's Return', and in the second act the growing enmity of the village and the final tragedy.

Sally Gilmour's impersonation of Tulip was astonishing. Even physically she managed to transform herself into a real native girl, spontaneous, innocent and reckless in her love for her husband and baby. Walter Gore was an authentic English sailor, and his sensitive understanding of his Tulip, his horror at the persecution roused against her and his loyalty in her defence were deeply moving. At the same time the life of the village was sketched with truth and humour. Tulip's delight at her first real European dress, the delicious scene in the inn when Tulip, once more in her native undress, dances to her husband's and his brother's delight, after the drunken villagers had retired – all this was full of life and truth. It made a tremendous impression and had splendid notices. When we showed this ballet in Melbourne later that year it had forty-three calls, no less. (I did not count them myself but it seems there are always some specialists who do!)

After a very brief holiday we embarked on the *Aquitania* to go to Halifax, Nova Scotia, at the end of August. The tables laden with white rolls and pounds of butter, and the rest of the rich food on board ship, were eagerly enjoyed by the whole company, after five years of war and the rationing that went on after it. From Halifax we flew to Chicago where Bentley Stone, a brilliant American dancer, who had appeared as guest with our company during our French tour, met us on a broiling hot day and took us straight away to eat ices in our first air-conditioned café. From there we flew on to San Francisco and the company embarked on the *Marine Phoenix* for the crossing to Sydney, while I remained for a week enjoying my first visit to America in that enchanting San Francisco. I stayed with a cousin of Ashley's whose wife belonged to a distinguished San Franciscan family, and we went out all the time meeting people who were very new to me, and delightful and amusing. I flew to Sydney, to arrive a week in advance of the company for preparation.

Just as we left San Francisco I saw the purser coming up to each passenger for a little talk, so I waited my turn, full of curiosity.

He took out of his pocket some stuff and handed it to me, and when I asked what it was, he said with a most reassuring smile: 'Oh, this is a shark repellent.'

Then he took out another little packet and said with a still broader grin: 'This is a colouring matter, you sprinkle it round you and it colours the water yellow so you are easier to spot from the air.'

However, all this did not spoil my enjoyment of the flight. We flew by night and rested in a hotel in daytime. The first day was in Honolulu. The intoxicating smell of pineapples right through the island made me realise I *was* in the tropics indeed. They put a *lei* of frangipani round my neck – a delightful custom – I felt positively drunk on the perfume. On the second or third day we stopped at Fiji for breakfast. I swallowed my coffee very quickly and rushed off to spend the remaining hour in doing a good vigorous practice as I felt numb with immobility. So I walked away from the airport and found something to hold on to for a barre. Happy to dance again, I forgot the time. Suddenly, an agitated Papuan with a huge mass of curly black hair standing on end and – most unexpectedly – in a policeman's uniform, arrived on a motor-bicycle and motioned me to get on to it. He spoke a lot but all I could make out was something that sounded like 'airport'. At the last minute my absence had been noticed at the airport and they were waiting for me to take off.

After three days I arrived in Sydney, where I was met by our impresario, did a broadcast and lunched with the manager of our theatre and some of the press. After lunch I flew to Melbourne, where sixteen bouquets awaited me at the hotel – I did not know a single giver, though! A conference with forty journalists proved how busy Mr O'Connor had been with advance publicity.

The company arrived a few days later, and we rehearsed for a week with ten Australian dancers who were added to bring up the number to forty.

We opened at the Princess Theatre in Melbourne and had the greatest reception of our lives. We did *Giselle* and *Gala Performance*. The audience was most excited, and we really did our best. There were no end of bouquets, one of them in the shape of a horseshoe big enough to frame me.

The press the next day was full of praise and we had full houses not only for the eight weeks which were scheduled, but for an additional eight weeks – so we danced there nearly four months, eight times a week.

We were all showered with flowers every night, most beautifully arranged in bouquets of all shapes. At first I used to stay about an hour after the show to pull out all the wires before putting the flowers into water. Then I found it too exhausting and one night just put the bouquet, wired as it was, into the fireman's pail of water. What a surprise it was three weeks later to find the flowers still fresh. The wire apparently fed the flowers with iron. Quite a useful thing to know in our profession!

After Melbourne we went to give three performances at Broken Hill, and visited the exciting silver mines there. I was given a piece of raw silver embedded in rock. Then to Sydney, originally booked for six weeks, but where we danced for three full months.

In March, towards the end of this run, I got a telegram from Ashley on our wedding anniversary ('Thirty years of happiness'), and I celebrated it by turning many of my best cartwheels on the stage.

In Sydney I stayed at a hotel near Bondi Beach and came to the theatre on a tram that brought me to the door. The manager used to give us a little supper after the performance was over. One night he had a party and I did not notice how the time was passing. Suddenly I realised that I had only a few minutes to dash to my dressing-room and change out of my evening dress into something suitable to wear in the tram. But all the lights in the theatre had been turned off at the main switch. The auditorium was in darkness and I couldn't have found my way to the dressing-room. Then a young man who knew the theatre well, said, 'Take my hand, and I'll lead you there.'

So he led me to my unlit dressing-room and I frantically started changing. At that time the fashion was for very narrow dresses, and as I tried to pull it off over my head, my dress stuck and I couldn't get out.

'I'm afraid I need your help, Harry,' I said. 'Will you come and pull upwards.'

So we both pulled, and as we were doing so all the lights suddenly went on again.

At Sydney there were great queues at the box office and I loved standing near by and hearing what the people said. I once heard a woman turn from the box office window, which she had just reached, and say to her husband: 'It's all right for Wednesday, Bill. Shall I book for Friday while we're about it?'

'No, Doris,' he replied. 'Let's get Wednesday over first.'

From Sydney we flew to New Zealand. In addition to the four principal cities Auckland, Wellington, Christchurch and Dunedin, in each of which we stayed for two or three weeks, we also went to smaller places and saw those marvellous geysers, and trout swimming in hot springs, and people cooking their dinner in the broiling earth.

In Wellington I spent a weekend at Government House as guest of that delightful pair Sir Bernard and Lady Freyberg, and did cartwheels all along an endless passage. When some years later I visited them in Windsor Castle, Lord Freyberg, as he was by then, asked me jokingly whether I still did cartwheels. I said I did and he became quite alarmed and begged me to desist.

In Christchurch I met that great woman Helen Keller. What an amazing character! Born blind, deaf and dumb, she has conquered all these handicaps in an almost supernatural way, and has achieved glory.

The Mayor of Christchurch invited me, together with four others, to meet her before the lecture she was giving in the Town Hall jointly with her marvellous friend Ethel Sullivan. At first, in the Mayor's parlour, when we were waiting for her, I expected an old blind woman, a sort of invalid. Then in came Helen Keller, a handsome woman, upright, well groomed, with a starched white blouse trimmed with lace and a pretty hat. She walked in without the slightest hesitation and greeted the Mayor who went towards her. After that he introduced each of the guests. When she came to me she slid both her hands over my face, brow, eyes and cheeks. And then she said to me (Ethel Sullivan translating) something so wonderfully comforting that I burst into tears and kissed her hands.

When she lectured she touched her friend's hand and by

imperceptible movements conveyed not only the sense, but the exact words she wanted to say. Afterwards we were invited to ask questions which she answered in the same way. It was a miraculous collaboration. Only when Helen Keller actually tried to *speak* and to say the words 'I love Christchurch' herself, that the terrible difficulty of her speech made me realise the magnitude of her victory.

She was the greatest woman I have ever met. Not only did she conquer her incredible combination of disabilities, but she wrote and translated several works and toured all over the world to raise funds for the disabled of all sorts, and above all to give courage to them by her marvellous example.

One day, when I was sitting in the dining-room of a hotel in Christchurch, I spotted Sir Bernard and Lady Freyberg, who had entertained me so kindly in Wellington. They asked me when I was returning there and offered to give me a lift in their plane. I had never been in a private plane before and accepted with alacrity. We were only six, including the pilot, and it was a delightfully gay flight, full of laughter.

From New Zealand we made a return visit of three weeks to Sydney. I was taken up to Bulli Pass, those marvellous mountains with the jungle on their slopes reaching down to the ocean. We saw a beach full of bathers, so I begged the old couple who drove me there to let me have a swim. I went to change in the huge bathing establishment, but when I came out there was nobody in the water all the bathers were on the beach. I did not feel very much like going in all alone, but as I did not wish to keep my friends waiting too long, I stepped into the sea. A strong man pulled me back and said:

'Didn't you hear the shark bell?'

For our return visit to Melbourne Gore did a new ballet *Winter Night* to Rachmaninoff's piano concerto, with designs by a talented young Australian, Kenneth Rowell. This was a way of repaying the marvellous reception that we had in

Australia. It was a lyrical work with dramatic overtones and blended perfectly with Rachmaninoff's music. The sets and costumes, simple and poetic, completed the mood.

We also produced there the second act of Tchaikovsky's *Nutcracker*, in which Belinda Wright and John Gilpin won the audiences with their new brilliance. She and John Gilpin had matured a great deal by then and danced many leading classical and romantic roles.

Our next date was Adelaide. I visited the vineyards belonging to my darling Sally Gilmour's husband – she had married at the end of our first year there. Belinda Wright was now dancing many of her parts.

Brisbane as well as Adelaide received us very warmly. From there we went to Perth in West Australia, our last city before embarking for home. In Perth I met Linley Wilson who had invited me to stay with her at our very first meeting. She was a remarkable teacher of ballet, married to Keith George, a man of great culture and with a passion for the theatre. It was from her school that I had later some excellent dancers. I also spent a week with them at their house at Gooseberry Hill, practically in the jungle, the wildest place I have ever been to – and it was like paradise. I ate peaches and apricots hot from the tree.

We danced four weeks in Perth, and at the last performance we had a delirious reception, with streamers thrown to us from the gallery, so we were linked with the audience, and among the masses of bouquets on the stage there was a boomerang made of flowers – a touching invitation for us to return.

We embarked on the *Arawa* for a five-week voyage. It was the most complete rest I have ever had – and I needed it badly after nearly eighteen months of very hard work. During the tour I had taken all the classes and rehearsals myself and been in the wings for every performance. In addition I had given as many as ten private lessons a week. *And* I had attended all the receptions. And laughed a lot. And cried a lot too. How I found the strength to keep all this up for eighteen months I shall never know.

Nevertheless, we practised and rehearsed *Winter Night* on the deck of the *Arawa*, as the ballet was very new and we were afraid of forgetting it.

All through that voyage I was resolved to brush aside thoughts of the bleak future. We had only one single engagement before us – a week at the Bath Festival. We had lost all touch with English theatres. Other companies had taken our dates as we had been absent so long, and it seemed as though Australia might keep us for good. In fact we had had some interesting offers, but in the end home drew us back. It is obvious now that we were managed shockingly badly by our own staff (Mr O'Connor, be it said, was perfect to the end). Our scenery was not packed properly, no bill of lading was given to me, so that I could hardly retrieve what in any case was no more than a quantity of backcloths and costumes ruined by abominably careless packing. And, although we had beaten all the records for takings, hardly any money had been sent to our account in England, in spite of repeated cables from Ashley to our business manager in Australia. A hideous awakening after that marvellous success. And we had left in Australia not only our beloved Sally Gilmour but other dancers too. And soon after our return John Gilpin and Belinda Wright joined Roland Petit's company – for I had very little to offer them at the time.

During our long absence in Australia we had of course no grant from the Arts Council. But on our return they gave us £500 to start again. Somehow we managed to prepare for Bath and also a visit to Belgium.

David Paltenghi, who had been a *premier danseur* of the Sadler's Wells Company and all through the war had the honour and joy to partner Margot Fonteyn, offered to join our company, not only to dance but also to do choreography. He had excellent ideas for ballets, and I had great hopes of him. But his talent was mainly for choice of themes, music and designs. In short his bent was for production, not actually for choreography, and so his ballets did not last in our repertoire. Of all his works the only thing that has lasted is a beautiful score for *Prologue to Canterbury* by Racine Fricker, with remarkable designs by Edward Burra. I hope we may have a chance to use them some day with new choreography.

In the meantime Gore wrote a striking ballet *Antonia*, with music arranged from Sibelius. This was a drama of jealousy in which Paula Hinton (later his wife) gave a really powerful performance as the cruel woman, and Gore as the tormented lover wrung one's heart. Gore had already treated the theme of jealousy in *Winter Night*, and later, in the sixties, he came back to it in *Night and Silence*. Of all the choreographers I know he is the most eloquent on the theme of love – he really is a poet of love – from his *Bartlemas Dances* (music by Holst) all gaiety and innocence, through the tenderness of the *Sentimental Sarabande* in *Simple Symphony*, the reckless love and jealousy of *Winter Night* and *Antonia*, to a perfect acceptance of jealousy as an inherent part of love in *Night and Silence*, his undoubted masterpiece.

His are real men and women, not the invented romantic creatures of the majority of ballets, which are found even in the would-be realistic theatre of today.

Antonia made a tremendous impression in Paris at the Sarah Bernhardt Theatre where we went for a fortnight in 1950. On the opening night we had given *Lady into Fox*, for Sally Gilmour had returned to us for that season. Unfortunately the orchestra disliked the transcription of the Honegger music (originally written for piano) and played it atrociously, so the ballet did not have its usual impact, in spite of Sally's brilliant performance. But the Tudor ballets provoked real enthusiasm.

Antonia was sensationally successful in Germany where that same year we made a second long tour. This time the Germans were already crowding the theatres – most of them newly rebuilt. We opened in Göttingen to enthusiastic audiences. University students in bacchic mood almost carried me in their arms. I treasure the ribbons of the bouquet I had from them on our first night. We all felt deeply the joy of being friends again after the ghastly war.

The Tudor ballets *Dark Elegies, Gala Performance* and *Judgement of Paris* were our greatest successes. *Gala Performance* had beautiful sets and costumes by Hugh Stevenson. It was about three ballerinas who come to dance as guests in a foreign capital, at about the end of the last century. They were the 'Reine de la Danse' from Moscow, the 'Déesse de la Danse' from Milan and the 'Fille de Terpsichore' from Paris. They vie with each other to win the favour of the public, each with her own special talents: the Moscow star with her endless pirouettes, the Milan one with her perpetual displays of balance, and the Parisian with her happy bouncing. She is the only good-natured one, the others are harpies, whose true nature is revealed at rehearsal, and they delude themselves into thinking that they can hide it from the audience at the performance. The relations between these ballerinas and the local cavaliers, whom they consider unworthy to partner them, and also with the willing but frightened *corps de ballet*, were subtly brought out and the result is excellent comedy as well as charming choreography.

The *Judgement of Paris* is also a comedy ballet, but more bitter. The title and the names of the three goddesses on the programme prepare one for a classical theme. Far from it, the curtain rises on a sordid little café and three tired prostitutes. They don't expect any more clients and walk off, but are immediately recalled by the dirty waiter when a very drunk customer walks in. They each do a routine of a different character. The first is a smart girl with a fan, which she wields coquettishly, and is very sure that she will win him – but she fails. The second is an indolent blonde, and her lazy dance with pink hoops is comic and seductive at the same time. The third one is getting on in age and fails to do what was her great trick – the splits. The blonde is chosen, but by this time the drunk is too drunk and they rob him. It ends with the blonde girl dropping his watch slowly into her bodice. Kurt Weill's music (from the *Dreigroschen Oper*) is a perfect accompaniment to the bitter humour of this ballet.

On that tour we visited several cities, all in the process of active rebuilding and teeming with theatrical life.

In Bonn I went to the Beethoven Museum. I was staggered to see the amount of hearing aids which Beethoven had used. I knew, of course, that he had been deaf and never heard his own Ninth Symphony, which he conducted. But somehow I thought that a composer heard the music in his imagination and that Beethoven was resigned not to hear it in reality. It was tragic to see how he longed for the *real* sound, and the dreadful primitive hearing aids – the only ones available then

78. One of my million cartwheels

79. Flying home on the ship from Australia (myself and John Gilpin)

80. Curtain call in Australia

81. With our distinguished hosts in China, 1957

82. On my eightieth birthday: Karsavina with the original Marie Rambert dancers: Howard, Schooling, Ashton, Rambert, Lloyd

83. Making them laugh for a group photograph

84. Norman Morrice

85. *Two Brothers*, Norman Morrice, Gillian Martlew, John Chesworth

86. The Directors watching
a rehearsal

87. Norman Morrice
rehearsing *That is the Show*,
with Jonathan Taylor,
Christopher Bruce and
Sandra Craig

88. Head of Rambert by Astrid Zydowa
(acquired by the National Portrait Gallery)

– that he had to use: things which resembled copper sauce-pans or frying-pans, three pedals to his piano in the hope of augmenting the sound – yet nothing could reach him. Terrible, terrible, that this should have happened to him – of all geniuses!

In Lübeck we saw most fascinating medieval mural paint-ings, and in another town glorious Memlings with extra-ordinary, precise details in the painting so that if you looked closely you could see each separate hair in a beard – yet this never disturbed the profound mood of piety in the picture.

The last week of that tour was in Berlin, where we danced at the Theater des Westens. The farewell performance was a matinée at eleven in the morning. Apparently in Russia too they do these matinées before lunch, but to us it seemed an unearthly hour and we dreaded spoiling a week of brilliant success with a sad finish. But we need not have feared. The mood of excitement was generated the minute the curtain rose. And when it fell we wished for many more such matinées.

We returned to London much refreshed by our continental experience. And again the exhausting round of provincial touring took up all our time and left hardly a moment for new works.

Fortunately at that time I was able to receive increasing help in organising from David Ellis, who was running his Ballet Workshop at the Mercury – which the Ballet Rambert had long outgrown. It was a joint enterprise with his wife, my daughter Angela, and they had founded the Workshop for the production of new ballets.

I began to depend more and more on David's help, and as he was finding it increasingly difficult to find new choreo-graphers, he decided to close his workshop and accept my invitation to become my Associate Director. By that time his Workshop had existed over four years, and had done very good work.

I was made a C.B.E. in 1953. When I received the letter from the Prime Minister I had no idea what C.B.E. meant. I was very excited when I knew I would receive it personally from the Queen, who had only just been crowned. Some time later when the Kirov company was in London, a few of their dancers came to see us rehearse at the Mercury. Seeing on the table a pile of writing paper with my name on it, one of the dancers asked me what those letters after my name meant. I stuck out my chest, put my thumbs in my armpits and said: 'I am a Commander of the British Empire!' 'Then the British Empire has nothing to fear!' he said with a wicked smile.

In 1955 we visited Northern Italy and appeared in Perugia, Bologna, Venice and other towns. In Venice our conductor fell ill and the resident conductor of the Fenice (what a glorious theatre!) conducted, unprepared, and flawlessly, John Cranko's ballet *Variations on a Theme* by Frank Bridge. That *was* an achievement!

The following year we did an exciting tour of Spain. We started with Valencia, Barcelona, Madrid and then appeared in open-air theatres all over the country. It was a very hot summer, and what a delight it was to dance in those fragrant, intoxicating groves. In practically every theatre we followed Antonio, that incomparable Spanish dancer, who was also touring then. We could not find a suitable actor to be the narrator in *Peter and the Wolf,* and so I learned the text in Spanish and spoke it apparently without accent. I was even invited to speak Spanish on the radio, but my vocabulary was restricted to the words of *Peter and the Wolf.*

Our next big tour was to China in 1957. We could hardly believe that such an extraordinary thing could happen to us until we had actually set off. I went by boat to Leningrad; I wanted very much to revisit it as well as Moscow. I boarded the *Baltika* at Tilbury. It was very comfortable, and I had a luxurious cabin which, I gathered, may have been Khrushchev's when he travelled on this ship. The food was delicious, and we had on board some twenty schoolboys in their finishing year from Gordonstoun, Eton and Harrow. We visited Stockholm and one or two other towns on the way.

Each time I see Leningrad I find it more beautiful than I had remembered. Surely it is the most aristocratic city in the world. Now that it is no more the seat of the government, it has lost the bustle and activity that go with being a capital city and is now unusually leisurely and elegant.

I travelled overnight to Moscow by train and on arrival was greeted – most unexpectedly – by Natalia Roslavleva. I had never met her before, but we had become friends by correspondence. She is a historian of ballet, and her book *The Era of Russian Ballet* contains an immense amount of facts of which previously we were quite ignorant. She took me to watch a class of the remarkable Stanislavsky ballet company. We also visited the Bakhrushin Museum and the University.

I went by the midnight plane to Irkutsk, where we were going to stay several hours before boarding a Chinese plane to Peking. I took a strong sleeping pill and told our Russian hostess not to disturb me at any of the intermediate stops, like Krasnoyarsk and Novosibirsk. However sonorous the name of an airport, what you see there is always the same. It was a small Russian plane (we had missed the TU 4) and I sat right in front alone. As I became drowsy, I stretched myself out on the other seat too, and when still more sleepy, I rolled willingly on to the floor. I don't know how long I had been sleeping when I felt somebody holding my wrist and heard in Russian: 'Her pulse seems quite all right.' So I had caused them some anxiety, but I think they allowed me to continue my blissful sleep on the floor.

In Irkutsk I was given a beautiful suite at the hotel, complete with Nottingham lace curtains as well as apple-green velvet ones, and even a plant on the writing-table – all practically a copy of my cabin on the *Baltika* – so there was no doubt they were treating me as a V.I.P., and some mighty personage must have occupied it before. From Irkutsk we flew to Peking on a small Chinese plane. We only stopped once, in Ulan Bator in Outer Mongolia, where to my surprise I saw a group of most beautiful Mongolian women right out of another century, waiting to *fly*.

We arrived in Peking at 1 p.m. on 8 September. The Chinese ballet company met us with bouquets for each of our dancers, including the embarrassed males. A woman came up to me and said, 'Don't you recognise me? I was your pupil in the thirties. How is Freddie, how is little Alicia, how is Antony Tudor?' I then recognised her, but could not remember her name. She told me it was Tai-ai-lien. 'But you called me Eileen for short,' she added.

She told me that after training at my school she had asked whether there was a chance of her joining my company. I told her at the time that if she were outstanding, and people noticed her for her qualities as a dancer I would certainly take her. But as she was only average, they would notice her for unimportant things like the difference in colour and features. I advised her to go back to China to teach, which she was excellent at, and perhaps found a company of her own. She did so at the outbreak of the 1939 war, and when Mao Tse-tung came into power he made her director of the National School of Ballet. It is housed in a simple but comfortable building, with at least six large studios and a big room in the basement, where a very skilful cobbler looking like a pixie makes ballet shoes for the whole school.

I watched a class which was taken by an excellent young teacher. When the school had been founded they invited teachers from the Bolshoi to train their teaching staff, and the results were remarkable. In the double work class I saw six handsome Chinese youths (taller than their average) supporting six beautiful girls in pirouettes and the great Soviet lifts. They did for me the *pas de deux* from *Swan Lake*. I asked Tai-ai-lien whether she intended to produce the European classics in the theatre. She said, 'Why not, if they dance them well enough. It is only necessary to make them up well. When *you* want to represent the Chinese on the stage, you paint their faces yellow, slant their eyes upwards and drop the corners of the mouth. When *we* want to represent Europeans, we paint ourselves white and reverse the lines for eyes and mouth! So why should we not do even *The Sleeping Beauty*?' I could not but agree with her.

I asked what was going to happen in that case to their own Chinese Classical Theatre, which we had seen in London the year before – it had been to us a revelation of completely new beauty. She took me to the next door in the studio. There standing at the barre the pupils were doing exercises of quite a special style, so that at the end of the training they could dance and preserve their most ancient dances. In the past they could only be transmitted from very old people to tiny children, who learned for years to break in their bodies into that very special style. As those old people died out, the source of that great knowledge was in danger of extinction. Now they have evolved a complete system of training, based on the deepest features of the Chinese tradition – and so it can be preserved just as our European tradition is.

I was most impressed by that wonderful school with its perfect curriculum and felt proud of my pupil – and, if the truth must be told, very envious of her opportunities, from the point of view of both personnel and all their resources.

We visited the Temple of Heaven and the Summer Palace – places I never dreamt I would see with my own eyes. The evenings when we were not dancing we went to the enchanting Peking Opera.

We stayed in a comfortable hotel, but we were amazed to find that there were no wardrobes in our rooms, only cupboards where you laid out your clothes. In each room there was a brush and comb, immaculately clean, and a pair of large bedroom slippers to fit any foot. Yet they have very small feet. We even saw some poor creatures with bound feet – but that was disappearing when we were there. Actually, I don't think that custom was any more barbarous than the European corset.

We went in rickshaws, drawn by men (mercifully on bicycles nowadays), and on three occasions I made myself understood by means of gesture alone: I bought stamps and asked for glue; I bought a silk dressing-gown; and I had a long mimed scene with a street cobbler. I wanted him to sew a strap on to a bag so that I could sling it from my shoulder. We both laughed a great deal when he understood and carried out the order perfectly.

I saw the great October celebration, most extraordinary processions of people performing plays and ballets, and even circus acrobatics, while keeping pace with the marchers.

On the first night we danced *Giselle*. The queues for it started two days before our arrival. The house was excited, and so were we, of course. But there was no applause after the first act, and we felt we had failed. However, in the interval some people came backstage full of enthusiasm. They told us they never applaud after the first act of *Giselle* as it has a corpse on the stage! Anyhow, after the second act there was delirious applause. Oh, how comforting!

For our second programme we did *Coppélia*. Chou En-lai came on the stage after the show and made a most amiable speech, which, translated, was word for word what I was briefed to say – that 'art knows no frontiers', 'artists are the best ambassadors' and so forth.

Our third programme, which was not a full-length ballet, was very much less of a success. We were relying on Gore's beautiful *Winter Night* and Tudor's *Gala Performance* as well as *Les Sylphides*. But like the Russians now, they only liked a full evening's classical ballet, and not a programme of one-act ballets, which they call miniatures, so we dropped them for the remainder of the tour and only did *Giselle* and *Coppélia*. We were wonderfully entertained by various organisations. Many members of the company even learnt to eat with chopsticks, and what's more, like virtuosos.

I did not stay the full two months in China and left the company in the care of my Associate Director, while I hastened to have a holiday in Greece.

I had never seen Athens. I stayed with Greek friends and was plunged into its beauty all day long. They knew every corner of the land and showed me everything during the fortnight I spent there.

I saw *Iphigenia in Tauris* in the Herodotus Atticus Theatre in the Parthenon. As with all great performances, the fact of not understanding the language did not prevent one from being deeply moved, and I wept at Iphigenia's very first words.

15

In 1959 we were invited to appear at 'Jacob's Pillow' near Boston. We had never performed in the United States before, though I knew South America from our Diaghilev tour.

Jacob's Pillow is run by Ted Shawn for long summer Dance Festivals, to which he invites interesting dance groups of most varied types – classical, contemporary, short ballets, concert numbers and so forth. During the day it is a kind of University of the Dance, with a choice of brilliant teachers, and in the evening there are performances in their delightful barn theatre. It was lovely to have Martha Graham and Agnes de Mille come and see us and renew our friendship.

I had first seen Martha Graham's company only a few years before and had been completely carried away, both by her choreography and by her impeccable dancing in her own idiom. The style was absolutely different from the classical style of ballet. In the balletic style you hold your back firm all the time, whatever you do with the body and the arms. In her case the back could alternately be completely firm or completely relaxed. This language had a great influence on many disciples of Martha who found through it their means of expression. In our company we teach her exercises alongside the classical ones, because they complement one another and form a richer dance vocabulary.

The classical ballet was born of the court, where the object of dancing was to show one's elegance and courtliness. While the peasants walked with their feet turned in under the weight of the burdens they had to carry, the courtier turned out his feet, kept his back straight and moved his arms gracefully. But Martha Graham's dancing had nothing to do with classical ballet. Perhaps Eastern dancing, which had influenced Ruth St Denis, may have been less alien to Martha's nature. But hers was above all the expression of a tormented soul. She threw herself on the ground and danced there no less than in the air. Her great influence on choreography of the twentieth century had created a completely new choreographic language.

Our greatest success in America was *Two Brothers*, a ballet produced that spring by our new choreographer, Norman Morrice. He had been in my school since 1951. Even in his first year he had felt a desire to try choreography. In fact, together with another pupil, he devised a school show in which they performed their little ballets. I thought their efforts worthwhile, and when the other boy told me of an idea he had for a new ballet I let him try it. The ballet did not confirm my first impression, and was soon dropped.

It was later that Morrice submitted an idea which appealed to us very much, and, as a result, he produced *Two Brothers* with music by Dohnani and sets and costumes by Ralph Koltai. This ballet showed a definite talent. The story is about two brothers of whom the older has a simple steady character, while the younger one is a complex, violent spirit. He falls in love with his elder brother's fiancée and subsequently kills him in a fit of fury. It was told with real understanding of the characters and situations, and deep sympathy. Choreographically the language was too restrained for the melodious Dohnani, and would have been more effective with a different type of music. But even so, the ballet had beautiful passages and interesting groups. It had an immediate appeal to the younger generation, and they surprised us all by storming the stage-door to see Norman Morrice. It created a real impact, and I was happy to find yet another important choreographer emerging from our group.

On the way back from America our company appeared in Baalbek, dancing against those fabulous ruins.

It was becoming more and more difficult to show any of our newer works – the cry was only for full-length classics. I decided to produce *La Sylphide* – a dream of mine since 1928 when Ashton, on returning from his engagement with the Ida Rubinstein company in Paris, brought me a small study on this ballet by Slonimsky, the famous Russian ballet critic.

I went to Paris in 1950 to see Harald Lander, who was then ballet master at the Grand Opéra, and try to persuade him to produce *La Sylphide* for us, as he had done the Danish version.

It was a fruitless visit, because Lander was too busy to help us, but I had one droll experience. I happened to be at the Place de l'Opéra, and I wanted to go to the Théâtre Marigny to give a private lesson to Colette Marchand. But it happened that Queen Juliana was paying a three-day state visit, and the perpetual traffic jams made circulation impossible, the cars could hardly move. So I thought this was a unique opportunity to take the horse cab which usually stood at the Opéra with its smart coachwoman in her elegant riding breeches and little bowler hat. I got in, feeling very grand in an open carriage, ready to wave my hand and pretend to be Queen Juliana herself. But the horse hardly advanced, and when we got to the Café de l'Opéra it stopped completely.

'What's the matter?' I said. 'Why doesn't your horse move?'

'Mon cheval désire uriner.'

So we had to wait. And suddenly there was a rush – a Niagara. I gave up all thoughts of being Queen Juliana, I didn't know where to hide.

La Sylphide was originally written for the great Taglioni by her father in 1832. It was the first truly romantic ballet and served as a pattern for all the subsequent romantic ballets. The theme was the conflict between the real world and the world of spirits. Here is the synopsis:

James, a Scots farmer, is betrothed to Effie. On the eve of

the wedding the Sylphide appears to him and he falls in love with her and she with him. Unlike Fokine's melancholy Sylphides, Bournonville's creation is a happy spirit of the air, rejoicing in her flights. Captivatingly naïve, when she sees James give Effie the ring, she tells him that she too would like a ring. In her efforts to win him she tells him that she owns all the forest, and when he remains downcast, she brings him down a bird's nest to amuse him. He tells her to let the imaginary bird fly away. She obeys, but is puzzled and sad. She flies away and he thinks it was only a dream.

The next day, when the wedding guests have assembled, James discovers Madge, the Witch, who has stolen in and mixed with the guests. He throws her out as he is sure she bodes no good. During a reel, in which all the guests take part, the Sylphide appears to James again and lures him away into the forest.

In the interlude after the first act Madge, together with other witches, is stirring a brew from which she draws a magic scarf. In the second act she gives this scarf to James, promising him that with it he will capture the Sylphide and hold her on earth. But when he ties her wings with the scarf they fall off and she dies. So the witch has had her revenge and James has lost both his earthly bride and the Sylphide.

We finally managed to produce that ballet in a perfect version by Elsa-Marianne von Rosen, with choreography by Bournonville, the great Danish master. We were all used to Petipa's style in *The Sleeping Beauty*, but Bournonville had entirely different accents. A jump would come at quite a different moment than Petipa had taught us to expect. This made it very difficult to dance, but also very fresh and new, in keeping with the originality of the touching story.

It was one of our greatest successes, yet did not draw the provincial public as we were hoping to, because they confused the name with *LES Sylphides*, which was danced by every company in London and all over the country. Yet it was *La*

Sylphide which was at the origin of Fokine's conception. In the first charity performance, which was in 1904, he did a series of separate subjects on each piece of Chopin's music that he had chosen. Thus the first Nocturne represented a procession of monks against the background of a ruined monastery; the two Mazurkas accompanied a Polish peasant wedding; and the Valse for the *pas de deux* was danced by Pavlova, dressed as La Sylphide (the Taglioni one) and partnered by Nijinsky. That dance was breathtaking, and Fokine then decided, possibly with the advice of Benois, to dress all the danseuses in the romantic dress with a long gauze skirt; and Nijinsky wore white tights, a white soft silk shirt with a floating white bow, and a black velvet waistcoat. Thus the Scottish farmer's costume became a romantic poet's one.

Les Sylphides, undoubtedly, is Fokine's masterpiece. We had it in our repertoire ever since it had been produced for us by Karsavina in 1930.

But, when we had to do away with our corps de ballet, I mourned the loss of our *La Sylphide*, which I love passionately, more than almost any other ballet in our repertoire.

And it all started with Ashton's little gift of the booklet on *La Sylphide* which he brought me from Paris in 1928!

Ashton has worked with the Royal Ballet over thirty years now. He is an inspired and prolific choreographer, and it would be impossible to enumerate even a few of his best ballets. My own preference is his *Symphonic Variations* to César Franck with one of the greatest décors seen in ballet. Sophie Fedorovitch painted a huge expanse of green with some vague black lines on top. When I asked her how this particular colour-scheme came to her, she said that whenever she drove in Norfolk (where she lived and which she loved) she always noticed the telephone wires patterned against the immense green fields. It was a daring thing for Ashton to have chosen to use only six dancers for this ballet, and he hesitated for a long time, but his decision was most happy, for the three couples disported themselves in that enormous space like birds in the sky. It was the *more* daring a thing to do, as it was his first ballet for the Covent Garden stage, and when he had at his disposal a very large company for the first time in his life.

Another ballet of his, which I consider a masterpiece, is his *Scènes de Ballet* to Stravinsky's music. It is also an abstract ballet, following very closely the music. Here the décor and costumes are most inappropriate, and I am sure this ballet would gain even if the dancers wore ordinary practice clothes, unless a new Sophie Fedorovitch could be born. Alas, that she had died – and by a tragic accident – in 1953.

La Fille Mal Gardée is a masterpiece of another kind, as in form it is a typical full-length classical ballet to the original score by Hérold, beautifully reworked by Lanchbery. Ashton tells the simple story very clearly through pure classical dance. Even the antics of the half-witted Alain are expressed by classical *enchaînements*. Yet it is all fresh choreography, never using any old patterns, always enchanting, and it exploits to the utmost the special qualities of the English – as opposed to Russian – dancers of our time. His is a restrained elegance in movement typical of English ballet. I doubt whether the Russians with all their brilliance would dance it as Ashton really wants. In the same way as the great classics of Petipa, written for Russian ballerinas, never had the same brilliance when danced even by the best English dancers, so Russian dancers will have the same difficulty in acquiring the Ashton style. He has written by the age of sixty-seven more than a hundred and thirty-five ballets – so he has beaten Petipa!

I had always been a great admirer of Balanchine's choreography, ever since he did his first work for Diaghilev which was *Barabau*. This was followed by a series of brilliant works, culminating with *The Prodigal Son* in the year of Diaghilev's death. An opportunity to include him in our repertoire came when he very generously released some of his ballets for reproduction outside his own company. He sent us John Taras – a distinguished choreographer himself – to teach us *Night Shadow*, an exquisite neo-romantic ballet with music by Rieti on themes by Bellini. The décor was by Alix Stone. There was a mysterious dance for the sleepwalker when she comes down in her nightgown holding a candle before her and glides, unseeing, on her points, while the poet attempts unsuccessfully to stop her.

When we were in China we saw a performance of *Don Quixote* by a Russian company from Novosibirsk. We were very struck by Gorsky's choreography, and on our return decided to produce it. But it took us over three years to find somebody who could teach us the choreography.

In the end it was not a Russian but a Pole, Witold Borkowski, who did it for us. We had beautiful scenery and costumes by Voytek. In particular the scene with the windmills was most imaginatively designed, and yet realistically enough constructed to allow for Don Quixote's battling with them.

The music is by Minkus, a name to frighten away the musicians of today, yet with an irresistible attraction for dancers. It has such a strong dynamic quality, the tunes are so simple and danceable that it is one of the most popular ballets in Russia. The *pas de deux* in the last act lends itself perfectly to a display of classical virtuosity.

The role of Don Quixote, though only a mimed one, was interpreted to perfection by John Chesworth. He made the noble character of the knight shine through all the comic situations – thus giving even more point to the comedy and making us love the unfortunate Don the more.

Lucette Aldous was brilliant as Kitry and positively dazzling in the last *pas de deux*.

The ballet was well received by the press, both in London and the provinces. But the provincial public, for whom we performed almost all the year round, was shy of new titles. They would always fill the theatre for *Swan Lake* or *Sleeping Beauty* – both of these inaccessible to us because of the large orchestra and company required. But titles like *Don Quixote* or *La Sylphide* conveyed nothing to them and did not draw, although those who came were invariably enthusiastic.

In 1962 I was made a Dame, much to my surprise. I felt greatly honoured and I was delighted to get a telegram from Sir Isaiah Berlin: 'Welcome to the ranks of the Anglo-Russian aristocracy.' But among my friends I referred to it as 'The Daming of the Shrew'. Ashley used often to call me a shrew – and indeed on occasions he had reason. Once I rebelled and said: 'What is the male of a shrew?' He answered indignantly: 'Nature has not created such a monster. But there can be a husband of a shrew – and he would be called a shrivett.'

Soon after my 'Daming' the company set off for Germany to make a film of *Coppélia*. When we reached Folkestone there were signs in French in the usual places. One of the girls pointed at one and said: 'Now we are all Dames.'

Not long ago I was invited to join eleven other Dames for a luncheon at the *Sunday Times*. When I asked why the lunch had been arranged, I was told quite simply: 'You are our best export.' Sybil Thorndike, who was there, of course, told us that a friend of hers, hearing of the occasion, asked: 'And what is the collective noun for Dames? A Dirge of Dames?' 'No fear,' she said, 'we are a Dazzle of Dames.'

In that same year, I was the subject of the television programme *This is Your Life*. I knew absolutely nothing about it in advance. My secretary told me only that I had been asked to do 'an interview' on television. They wished to do the first few minutes in the print room at the Mercury, which is five minutes from my house. As the weather was appalling – melting snow, and dirty underfoot – a friend came to fetch me with a car. I did not know what I was to wear for the interview, so I took a case with me containing an evening dress, a day dress and some practice clothes. To be ready to change quickly, I did not trouble to do up the zip of the dress I was wearing. What was my surprise when the door of the print room was opened for me and I saw Eamonn Andrews, the producer, and a team of technicians under blazing lights, all ready to shoot. I got very angry and would have been very rude to them for giving me this abominable surprise, as I was not fit to be seen, in my huge snow-boots, with a thick mohair scarf wrapped round my head. But then Eamonn Andrews put a big card in front of my eyes on which was printed 'This is Your Life!' Until that moment the secret had been kept from me most scrupulously, the whole point of the programme being that the 'victim' had no idea of what was going to happen. I began to unwind my hideous mohair scarf, then feverishly tried to zip up my dress – all of which was later seen on the screen. It turned out to be one of the happiest events of my life.

The programme was shown that evening, and after the incident at the Mercury I had to promise not to divulge the secret. My secretary was allowed to ring a few of my friends and advise them to watch television that night, but under no circumstances reveal my name.

For the programme proper I was called on the stage and took a seat. Presently Karsavina appeared, said a few sweet things about me, kissed me and disappeared. Then came Ashton – same procedure. Then my adored Sally Gilmour, who had been flown from Melbourne the previous night specially for the programme. Then the old lady, over ninety years of age, who had been my first accompanist in 1906. John Gilpin and Belinda Wright appeared. Then there was a shot of the Metropolitan Theatre in New York, and I heard Antony Tudor's voice saying some kind words. Then Celia Franca's voice – also one of my artists – from Montreal. Then the voice of my younger daughter. She was living in Trinidad at the time – and I was thrilled to hear her. But Eamonn Andrews told me to look round – and there she was, large as life and smiling. She also had been flown in specially for that programme. Then there was a shot of the jungle in South Africa and Peter Scott with a little bird in his hand, talking to me and reminding me how I had taught him to do cartwheels when he was my pupil during the first war. He added: 'I believe I could still do them, shall I try?' and promptly executed a couple of perfect ones. It was all incredibly exciting and at moments very moving.

After the performance they gave me a supper party with all the people who had been brought together for the occasion. As I was walking in on Eamonn Andrews's arm, I whispered to him: 'Is it not marvellous that you, who had never met me before, should have had it in your power to make me so happy?' He tapped me on the shoulder and said laughing: '*And* earn my living at the same time.'

It's strange to recall my first experience of television, which was at Alexandra Palace – the 'Ally Pally' as I think of it – and that must have been in 1932 or 1933. There were only about twelve square feet in which to dance, so I arranged the *Minuet in G* by Beethoven for two dancers. (One of them was Hugh Laing, who later became a great star in the States.) The lights flickered blindingly, and we could hardly see each other. We never saw the result, but they seemed quite pleased with it.

Norman Morrice continued to produce one new work every year – it seemed impossible to find time for more rehearsals, yet he always was full of ideas for new works.

He did *A Place in the Desert* to music by Surinac. It had one or two striking moments and right through an atmosphere of biblical simplicity. His next ballet, to music by Bloch and décor by Ralph Koltai, was called *Conflicts*. It was about the conflict arising between a choreographer and his dancers who, while interpreting the characters which he wishes to create, become involved in their real relations with each other. He has moments of despair when he feels that human material is too difficult to wield as an instrument of art – but he is human himself, and in the end must accept.

We were invited to appear at the Festival of Spoleto, organised by Gian Carlo Menotti, and undertook to produce for them a new work by Morrice, *The Travellers*. The music was specially written by Salzedo and the designs were by Ralph Koltai. It told of a company of dancers who alight from a plane in a foreign country which has very strict laws unknown to them. At first it amuses them to defy these laws, but the most adventurous of them is caught and brainwashed. When he is at last released all spirit has gone out of him, and he is now the first to bow down to any order.

The choreography, though highly stylised, was most expressive and the ballet very moving. We did *The Travellers* in a programme with Morrice's *Conflicts* and Tudor's *Gala Performance*. The heading of the notice in the paper next morning was 'Tre capo di lavoro' ('Three masterpieces') – so of course we were highly elated. It completed our delight in living for ten days in that enchanting little town, very Italian and unspoiled.

That same year we had our wonderful tour of the Near East, including Greece, Persia, Cyprus and Egypt. It was a great joy to me to take the company to the Parthenon, which I knew from my previous visit, and we breathed the honeyed air amongst those miracles of the human spirit and hand. I never cease to marvel how even a small fragment of that sculpture, an arm, or even part of an arm, breathes life. Can we still do that?

We went several more times to the Parthenon, and each time it appeared more glorious. It is impossible to imagine all those wonderful statues when they were painted in glowing colours as they were originally, and of which we can still see the traces here and there. Might they have been even more beautiful then? Yannis Metsis, who had been my pupil and artist in our company and was now living and dancing in his native Athens, offered to take us to the Parthenon, of which he knew every stone. But when we came there, and he started showing us round, some professional guides attacked him, almost with blows for depriving them of their job. So we had to listen to their loud machine-made explanations, which were drowning Yannis's inspired whisperings.

In Salonika we were fascinated by the Turkish quarter as well as the Byzantine cathedrals, which are so unlike any we know from the West.

In Tehran I stayed with my old friends the Arfas, a remarkable couple. I first knew her as Hilda Bewicke when we were together in Diaghilev's company. Later, during the war we danced together with Lydia Kyasht in England.

Hilda was a soloist of distinction and she even took over Nijinska's place in *Faune* and *Carnaval*. After the war she rejoined Diaghilev and met, while dancing in Monte Carlo, a young officer in the Persian Army, Hassan Arfa. It was a *coup de foudre* between Hassan and Hilda. They married immediately and have lived in Tehran ever since.

Hassan wrote a most interesting book, *Under Five Shahs*. He is a born soldier, it is his true vocation, the only man I know who can speak of soldiering with the passion of an artist. He described in a fascinating way his experiences, and you feel steeped in Iran while reading the book.

The Shah and the Empress came with many of their court to our first night, and I could not believe it was true. The word Shah had always been associated in my mind with *A Thousand and One Nights* and suddenly to find myself presenting each member of my company to the Shah was beyond belief.

English touring, which followed, seemed even less exciting than before. The rehearsals were mainly for the replacement of artists – with perpetual travelling there always were some

– and it was difficult to snatch the time to rehearse Morrice's new ballet *Realms of Choice* for presentation at our annual season at Sadler's Wells. That ballet with music by Leonard Salzedo (subsequently our conductor) had a décor by Nadine Baylis. It was her first collaboration with Norman Morrice, and many followed. She has a rich imagination controlled by an always sober form and obtains the most unusual effects by deceptively simple means.

It was becoming obvious that the lack of a London home was an insuperable obstacle to any creative work.

We have a very good site for a theatre, more than half an acre of ground which Ashley had acquired as far back as 1936. It is opposite our old Mercury Theatre, which we long ago outgrew as a company, but which is occupied by the Rambert school under the direction of my daughter, Angela Ellis.

Ashley had given that site to The Mercury Theatre Trust, and we tried for a long time to find some other company to share the future theatre with us and join us in an appeal for public funds. Peter Hall of the Royal Shakespeare Theatre was very interested, and they even went so far as to commission Sir Basil Spence to draw up plans for a theatre and studios suitable for both companies.

Just as we were about to launch our joint appeal at a great dinner at Hampton Court (lent by the Queen for a celebration of Shakespeare's quatercentenary), the Barbican Trust offered to build a theatre for the Shakespeare Company to their own specifications, at the Barbican. That was a much more practical scheme for them as there would be no need to raise a fund for building, and they would only have a yearly rent to pay. They decided to accept it, and amicably invited us to join them. But the Barbican was altogether unsuitable for us, and so, though we were deeply grateful, we had to decline.

There was another scheme to make us join a big commercial ballet company and take over the artistic direction to raise its standards. After a long period of parleying we found the scheme unworkable. So three years were wasted trying to prepare the company for a bigger organisation, and David Ellis, who had put all his energy into that endeavour, decided to resign.

At that time Norman Morrice had the idea of re-forming the company by dismissing the *corps de ballet* (so indispensable in the classics, and so costly in travelling) and keeping only the soloists. He laid before me a plan so intelligent, practical and in accordance with our artistic ideals that I forthwith appointed him my Associate Director, a post he fulfilled to perfection for four years. Only now, in 1971 has he consented to become a full Director provided I also remain one. We appointed John Chesworth Associate Director.

Morrice does all the directing now, helped by John Chesworth, and I, when asked for criticism, can only find occasion happily to approve. Our respective roles were well defined by the *New York Times* when it said our company was now *orientated* by Rambert and *directed* by Morrice.

At the time when we re-formed the company in 1966 John Chesworth had been with me both as pupil and member of the company for over sixteen years. He is a remarkable artist in character roles. In fact, apart from Koren's Mercutio in Lavrovski's *Romeo and Juliet*, I have never seen such depth of interpretation as Chesworth's. In *A Place in the Desert* he was a real biblical patriarch. His Don Quixote was truly worthy of Cervantes. And in *Dark Elegies* his restrained grief tore one's heart.

Morrice had produced eight ballets before we re-formed the company. Since then he can hardly find time to compose new works, because of the very heavy task of directing, and also his desire to encourage other members of the company to choreograph.

Of Morrice's latest works *Blindsight* has been acclaimed as a very important work, combining, as it does, a profound theme with brilliantly inventive choreography. But it is with the powerful *That is the Show* that he has proved himself a master.

In our company the dancers have all the same status. They interchange parts and enrich every aspect of a role. Under Morrice's inspired direction a new group of choreographers is emerging among them. He fosters their creative spirit and gives me faith in the future – whether I look on or not.

AFTERWORD

I CANNOT finish this book without some general reflections
on the art of ballet. These thoughts came into my head in the
Parthenon, and since then have agitated me constantly. I think
that they pose a very important problem. The idea is quite
clear in my mind, but words refuse to order themselves into
simple clear phrases. But I must try.

In classical Greece painting, sculpture and architecture
were always united in a perfect synthesis. Since then each one
of these arts has become independent of the others and developed its own laws in the expression of a different domain of
the human spirit.

In the theatre too, three Muses were always united – poetry,
music and dance. Poetry was the first one to free herself and
develop her own rhythms, entirely unlike those of music, and
her own numerous forms. I imagine that music was the next
Muse to free herself from the customary association with
poetry and dance.

Works of art that are not static in time require notation.
Painting and sculpture do not – they exist as they are created.
But music, dancing and poetry must be notated, written down
in order to last. Probably the notation of music was invented
much later than the alphabet, which allowed the art of words
to develop new and independent forms. To choose out of the
welter of sounds in nature the basic ones that could form a
scale must have taken centuries. But as soon as that was
achieved, and it became possible to write down music, there
appeared composers who could express all they wanted

through pure music – without words, without dance. And so
orchestral music was born – the most abstract art existing. Of
course music with words did not become extinct; on the
contrary it reached great heights in forms such as opera and
oratorio.

Is the art of dance really an equal to that of music and
poetry, or is it a derivative art? When a choreographer has an
idea for a ballet, the first thing he does is to find music suitable for it, so that he can compose sequences of movements
and fix them in the memory of his dancers by the association
with the musical phrase. Thus, his work is mainly an illustra-
tion. In the case of great choreographers his work can become
an illumination, as in Balanchine's works to Stravinsky; or in
Ashton's to César Franck; or in Tudor's *Dark Elegies* to
Mahler's *Kindertotenlieder*. But when watching these ballets we
always hear the music too – so even if the music is specially
written to the choreographer's requirements it still is the composer's invention that creates the atmosphere and rhythmic
pattern of the ballet. We can listen to *Agon*, and *Kindertotenlieder* and Franck without the ballet, and be transported. But
we don't perform these ballets without music. It is an art that
hardly exists yet. Would even the best ballets we know make
their appeal if we saw them in silence without the underlying
music? There are some amongst the musical public who only
go to opera, others who only go to concerts. They don't want
to see, they close their eyes to hear the better.

Nowadays, when many choreographers begin to create a
few silent phrases in a ballet composed to music, one suddenly
realises how much more clearly one *sees* when not lulled by
hearing.

This problem is nearing solution because there exists at
last a notation of dancing – in fact there are two systems; the
older one called Labanotation, invented by Laban, used mostly
in America, and the Benesh system used in England and
Europe generally. Attempts to write down movement have

been made in the seventeenth century and even earlier, but at that time they could only write down simple sequences of Court dances made of very primitive steps.

I think that when the notation of movement becomes as natural a subject of study for dancers as writing music for musicians, there will emerge choreographers who will feel the need to express themselves completely on their own without borrowing even a part of their inspiration from music.

I know that the very thought of dance without music horrifies many people. But in antiquity unpainted statues would also have horrified the onlookers, because to them they looked like corpses. And so they painted them as realistically as they could. Yet it was only when sculpture dissociated itself from painting and architecture that each one of them became an independent art, capable of expressing on its own all the artist wished to communicate.

When I first mentioned dance as an independent art, as self-sufficient as music (which I asserted in my school essay at Dalcroze's in 1910 and which so exasperated him), I could not foresee that in my lifetime this idea would come so close to realisation.

Yet already in the sixties I have seen Jerome Robbins's masterly work, *Moves*, which is danced in complete silence; and you absorb every movement to the full, just as at a concert you absorb music pure, without realistic theme, without words, without décor. I saw *Moves* again in 1971, and the audience watched breathlessly and broke out in unrestrained applause.

I have also seen Walter Gore's *Eaters of Darkness*, a beautiful ballet he originally created to music by Poulenc. When it was in his programme at the Edinburgh Festival, he was not allowed to use the tape recording – so he risked performing it in complete silence. The effect was powerful and the whole audience was obviously deeply moved. I asked Gore how he managed to keep everything in time without music, since the pattern had been dictated by Poulenc (unlike the case of *Moves* which was composed to Robbins's own counts). Gore told me he had dressed himself as one of the crowd, and so managed to guide them. This ballet, unlike *Moves*, had a very dramatic theme which held the audience deeply interested in the drama itself. So here are two examples of ballet without music.

More and more choreographers of today compose short passages without music, and in general they are moving away from the Dalcrozian ideal of following the score exactly to the more individual way of fusing it, as an atmosphere in which the dancers move freely. Sometimes when the music stops and the movement continues in silence, one's attention to movement itself is stimulated by the change in atmosphere. Usually, though, at a good ballet, one, as it were, 'hears with the eyes and sees with the ears' – and it is a delicious sensation – so long live ballet *with* music! I would not for the world do without the form of ballet accompanied by sound, like the masterpieces of Petipa and Fokine, of Ashton and Balanchine and the younger school.

I am sure that there will always be choreographers who will write beautiful ballets with music, and I shall welcome them. But just as in music we can have many forms, such as opera, or oratorio, or symphony or any other form, so I would like dance to develop her own forms: epic, or lyrical, or abstract, or dramatic, or humorous. It is still far away, but it is coming.

Today a poet needs only a paper and pencil to say what he wants; a composer needs almost as little, and perhaps a piano as well. But a choreographer today needs all the paraphernalia of a company, and a studio, and some musical accompaniment.

Only when writing movement has become a matter of course for the choreographer, just as the writing of music is to the composer, will he be able to say all he longs to express –

in pure movement – resulting from his *own* experience of life, of happiness and misery, of depression and elation, of matter and spirit. And only then will my muse Terpsichore be the equal of her noble sisters.

INDEX

INDEX

Sylphides, Les, D 56, 60; BC 132–3; BR 198, 204; Symphonic Variations, RB 146, 204; Tale of a Lamb, The, 133; Tartans, The, BR 156, 165; Thamar, D 78; That is the Show, BR 213; Tragedy of Fashion, A, BC 119–22, 131, 134; Train Bleu, Le, D 121; Travellers, The, BR 210; Two Brothers, BR 201; Valentine's Eve, BR 156, 165; Valse Finale, BR 165; Variations on a Theme, 194; Winter Night, BR 187–8, 189

'Ballets 1933', 152
Barney, Natalie, 34–5
Basil, Colonel de, 158
Bath, 95
Bath Festival, 189, 190
Bauchant, 129
Baylis, Nadine, 212
Beecham, Sir Joseph, 58
Beecham, Sir Thomas, 146
Beethoven, Ludwig van, 39, 181, 192–3; Minuet in G, 209; Ninth Symphony, 192
Behrend, Mr and Mrs Louis, 168
Belgium, 190
Benesh, Rudolf, 216
Benois, Alexandre, 66, 82
Benois, Nadia, 146, 160, 164, 166, 176, 204
Bergson, Henri, 81
Berlin, 54, 113, 178–9; Reichstag, 179. See also theatres
Bernard, Jean-Jacques, 168
Bewicke, Hilda, 79, 91, 98, 99, 211
Birley, Rhoda, 110
Birmingham, 180. See also theatres
Blackpool, 130
Blake, William, 134
Blanch, Lesley, 152–3
Blasis, Carlo, 103
Bloch, Ernest, 209–10
Bolshoi company, 43, 138, 154, 180, 181, 196; London visit (1969), 59
Bonn: Beethoven Museum, 192
Borkowski, Witold, 206
Borodin, Alexander, 59
Bournemouth, 99
Bournonville, August, 203

Bowen, Harold, 80
Bowen, Vera, see Donnet, Vera
Boyce, William, 156, 165
Bridge, Frank, 194
British Drama League, 153
Britten, Benjamin, 180
Brockwell Park, 172
Brown, Ivor, 32
Brown, Pamela, 168
Browne, E. Martin, 166
Brussels, 114, 177
Budapest, 55
Buenos Aires, 75, 77
Bull, Peter, 168
Bulli Pass, 186
Burra, Edward, 190

Calais, 83, 114, 177
Camargo Society, 134, 136. See also under ballets (C)
Cambridge. See under theatres
Cannes, 38
cats, 174–5
Cecchetti, Enrico, 18–19, 43, 55, 59, 65, 72, 80, 118, 126; in London, 102–4, 106
Chabrier, Emmanuel, 157
Chaliapine, F., 66, 84
Chamberlain, Neville, 168
Chappell, William, 127, 132, 146, 152
Charrington, Nora, 116
Chekhov, Anton, 53
Chekrigin, 155
Chesworth, John, 206, 213–14
Chicago, 183
Chirico, Giorgio de, 127
China, 194, 196–9, 206
Chinese ballet company, 196
Chopin, Frédéric, 36, 40, 56, 59, 60, 99, 204
Christchurch, 186–7
Chu-Chin-Chow, 110
Churchill, Diana, 85
Churchill, Sir Winston, 85
Clare, Mary, 100
Clemenceau, Georges, 42
Cochran, C. B., 91
Cochran, Peggy, 133
Cocteau, Jean 87, 89

INDEX

INDEX

INDEX

INDEX

INDEX

INDEX

INDEX